1st EDITION

Perspectives on Diseases and Disorders

Asthma

Clay Farris Naff
Book Editor

PERSPECTIVES
On Diseases & Disorders

GALE
CENGAGE Learning

Detroit • New York • San Francisco • New Haven, Conn • Waterville, Maine • London

Christine Nasso, *Publisher*
Elizabeth Des Chenes, *Managing Editor*

© 2010 Greenhaven Press, a part of Gale, Cengage Learning

Articles in Greenhaven Press anthologies are often edited for length to meet page requirements. In addition, original titles of these works are changed to clearly present the main thesis and to explicitly indicate the author's opinion. Every effort is made to ensure that Greenhaven Press accurately reflects the original intent of the authors. Every effort has been made to trace the owners of copyrighted material.

Cover image copyright Marin, 2009. Used under license from Shutterstock.com

LIBRARY OF CONGRESS CATALOGING-IN-PUBLICATION DATA

Asthma / Clay Farris Naff, book editor.
   p. cm. -- (Perspectives on diseases and disorders)
Includes bibliographical references and index.
ISBN 978-0-7377-4551-1 (hardcover)
1. Asthma--Popular works. I. Naff, Clay Farris.
RC591.A7236 2009
616.2'38--dc22

2009023047

Printed in the United States of America
1 2 3 4 5 6 7 13 12 11 10 09

CONTENTS

David A. Cramer, Teresa G. Odle, and Tish Davidson

Asthma, a chronic inflammatory disease of the lungs, has many facets: varying severity levels, different treatment options, and a wide range of people who suffer from it.

USA Today Magazine

A wide variety of causes lie behind asthma. An attack can be provoked by a number of triggers, including such things as allergies, pollution, exercise, or weather conditions.

Cleveland Clinic

The symptoms of asthma—wheezing, coughing, and general breathing difficulties—are fairly easy to identify in a patient. Diagnosis, however, is more complicated.

National Heart, Lung, and Blood Institute

The treatments for asthma are as different as the people who suffer from the disease. Finding the right management strategy for each patient is vital.

CHAPTER 3   Personal Experiences with Asthma

FOREWORD

"Medicine, to produce health, has to examine disease."
—Plutarch

Independent research on a health issue is often the first step to complement discussions with a physician. But locating accurate, well-organized, understandable medical information can be a challenge. A simple Internet search on terms such as "cancer" or "diabetes," for example, returns an intimidating number of results. Sifting through the results can be daunting, particularly when some of the information is inconsistent or even contradictory. The Greenhaven Press series Perspectives on Diseases and Disorders offers a solution to the often overwhelming nature of researching diseases and disorders.

From the clinical to the personal, titles in the Perspectives on Diseases and Disorders series provide students and other researchers with authoritative, accessible information in unique anthologies that include basic information about the disease or disorder, controversial aspects of diagnosis and treatment, and first-person accounts of those impacted by the disease. The result is a well-rounded combination of primary and secondary sources that, together, provide the reader with a better understanding of the disease or disorder.

Each volume in Perspectives on Diseases and Disorders explores a particular disease or disorder in detail. Material for each volume is carefully selected from a wide range of sources, including encyclopedias, journals, newspapers, nonfiction books, speeches, government documents, pamphlets, organization newsletters, and position papers. Articles in the first chapter provide an authoritative, up-to-date overview that covers symptoms, causes and effects, treatments, cures, and medical advances. The second chapter presents a substantial number of opposing viewpoints on controversial treatments and other current debates relating to the volume topic. The third chapter offers a variety of personal perspectives on the disease or disorder. Patients, doctors, caregivers, and loved ones represent just some of the voices found in this narrative chapter.

Each Perspectives on Diseases and Disorders volume also includes:

- An **annotated table of contents** that provides a brief summary of each article in the volume.
- An **introduction** specific to the volume topic.
- Full-color **charts and graphs** to illustrate key points, concepts, and theories.
- Full-color **photos** that show aspects of the disease or disorder and enhance textual material.
- **"Fast Facts"** that highlight pertinent additional statistics and surprising points.
- A **glossary** providing users with definitions of important terms.
- A **chronology** of important dates relating to the disease or disorder.
- An annotated list of **organizations to contact** for students and other readers seeking additional information.
- A **bibliography** of additional books and periodicals for further research.
- A detailed **subject index** that allows readers to quickly find the information they need.

Whether a student researching a disorder, a patient recently diagnosed with a disease, or an individual who simply wants to learn more about a particular disease or disorder, a reader who turns to Perspectives on Diseases and Disorders will find a wealth of information in each volume that offers not only basic information, but also vigorous debate from multiple perspectives.

INTRODUCTION

In the fall of 2008, the joy of Thanksgiving suddenly turned to concern for the Scott family of Baltimore. Their nine-year-old son, Anthony, had been suffering from a cold. The young African American seemed fine as the Thanksgiving meal began, according to his mother, but developed troubling symptoms as the meal went on. Anthony began wheezing and panting.

Then he had trouble taking a breath. Alarmed, his parents took him to Johns Hopkins Children's Center, but despite the best treatment the doctors there could provide, Anthony died.

With his passing, Anthony joined an alarming number of children to fall mortal victim to the most common chronic childhood disease in America. According to the U.S. Centers for Disease Control and Prevention, 6.5 million American children suffer from asthma. That amounts to 9 percent of American youth, a figure that has more than doubled since 1980.

Asthma is a somewhat mysterious inflammation of the tiny airways in the lungs. As inflammation sets in, the airways constrict or become blocked altogether. Many triggers for asthma have been identified, but its root causes are an unsolved puzzle.

It is well established, for example, that asthma in children is strongly associated with allergies. However, many children who have allergies never develop asthma, and some children who have asthma do not suffer from allergies.

Psychologist M. Banks Gregerson of the Family Therapy Institute of Alexandria, Virginia, observes, "Millions worldwide have asthma, with the numbers succumbing

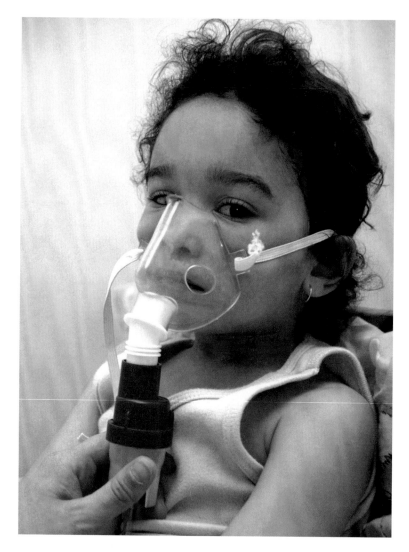

Though asthma in children is associated with allergies, many children with allergies never have asthma and some with asthma do not suffer from allergies. (© Angela Hampton Picture Library/ Alamy)

increasing sharply in the past two decades. After 2000 years of scientific study, who succumbs to asthma when is as puzzling as who regains health when and how."[1]

Higher Risk for African Americans

One thing is clear from the statistics: Anthony Scott of Baltimore fit the profile of the children most at risk. For reasons that remain obscure, African American children have a fivefold greater risk of asthma than white children.

The disparity in risk of death from the disease is even greater for young children. A 1993 government study showed that among children aged zero to four years, blacks were six times more likely to die from asthma than whites. Among older children, the disparity narrowed somewhat, but even so, African American children aged five to fourteen were four times more likely than whites of the same age group to die of asthma.

Scientists have speculated that genetic differences may be responsible for higher asthma risk among African Americans. Researcher Kathleen C. Barnes and her colleagues note: "Although it is not known to what extent genetic susceptibility contributes to asthma-related disparities, differences according to ethnicity in linkage and association studies between asthma and associated traits and genetic markers have been observed . . . suggesting distinct genes may be acting in different groups. . . ."[2]

However, while genes very likely play a role in who gets sick with asthma and how severe their disease becomes, that cannot be the whole explanation. Other studies of children in urban environments have found that Hispanic kids have the same or greater risk, yet their relevant genetic markers differ. Yet white children in the same urban setting seem to have somewhere between half and two-thirds the level of asthma risk. How can that be accounted for?

Researchers observe that one significant difference is family income. A much greater proportion of minority children live in poverty, and that alone may account for much of their susceptibility. Precisely why remains hard to explain.

Smoking Raises Asthma Rates

One key factor may be higher smoking rates among poor people. Tobacco smoke has been shown to trigger asthma, even among nonsmokers who simply share living space with a smoker. Not only is poverty more prevalent among African American and Hispanic households, but their smoking rates are higher as well. In 2006 about 5.8 million African American adults, or 22.6 percent, smoked cigarettes, compared with 21.8 percent of non-Hispanic whites. Hispanics generally have lower smoking rates, but these rates vary among them according to national origin. Puerto Ricans have some of the highest smoking rates and some of the highest asthma rates as well.

Young Anthony Scott was at risk for another reason besides his racial origins. Just living in an urban environment seems to increase the chance of contracting asthma. The obvious explanation is air pollution, which tends to be associated with urban environments. A decade-long study sponsored by California's Air Review Board found that pollution not only aggravates existing childhood asth-

Studies have shown that air pollution particles aggravate existing childhood asthma and may be one of the causes of asthma. (© mediacolor's/ Alamy)

ma but may actually be one cause of the life-threatening disease.

Several different types of pollution are suspected. Tiny particles suspended in the air, ozone, and nitrogen oxides may all contribute to the rise of childhood asthma. Yet there seem to be other factors at work in the urban/rural split. City children spend the vast majority of their time indoors, whereas rural children spend a good deal more of their time outdoors. This has led to studies of whether indoor air might be responsible for asthma. A number of studies have found evidence of a link.

The Hygiene Hypothesis

To make matters even more confusing, some medical researchers hypothesize that one reason for the rise of childhood asthma is that the modern urban home is too clean. The logic behind this involves the immune system. In a young child the immune system needs to be stimulated by exposure to a wide variety of pathogens and harmless substances before it can distinguish threats in the environment. The "hygiene hypothesis" holds that excessively sterile urban environments are depriving children of that exposure, leading to the development of allergies, which in turn are strongly associated with the development of childhood asthma.

Last in the list of asthma mysteries is that not all cases arise in childhood. In fact, about half of childhood cases disappear by adulthood, and then a smaller number of adults who never experienced asthma suddenly develop the disease. In a large portion of adult-onset cases, allergies are to blame. However, asthma can also follow from a bout of bronchitis, hormonal changes, or obesity. Even exercise can induce asthma.

Treatments Are Improving

This constellation of causes continues to puzzle medical researchers. "We don't know why some people get it and others don't," says Neil Schachter, a lung specialist at Mount Sinai Medical Center in New York City. "We know risk factors and predisposing factors, but we really don't have a full, fundamental understanding of why people develop asthma. We don't know how much is nurture, how much is nature."[3]

Fortunately, even though the reasons for the rise of asthma continue to be elusive, scientists are making progress in treating the disease. In the past, doctors could only react to the symptoms of an attack. Now, long-term medicines are helping to prevent an attack or at least mitigate the symptoms when one occurs. Such progress is saving lives.

Tragic though Anthony Scott's death was, he is among a dwindling number of children to succumb to the fatal potential of the disease. Asthma death rates for children have fallen from 3.0 deaths per 1 million children under age eighteen in 1999 to 2.5 deaths per 1 million in 2004. Before long, doctors and researchers hope, no child will have to die from the effects of asthma.

Notes

1. M. Banks Gregerson, "The Curious 2000-Year Case of Asthma," *Psychosomatic Medicine,* vol. 62, 2000, p. 816.
2. Kathleen C. Barnes, Audrey V. Grant, Nadia N. Hansel, Peisong Gao, and Georgia M. Dunston, "African Americans with Asthma: Genetic Insights," *Proceedings of the American Thoracic Society,* July 2007, p. 58.
3. Quoted in Carol M. Ostrom, "Asthma Is on the Rise but Remains a Mystery," *Seattle Times,* January 5, 2005. http://community.seattletimes.nwsource.com/archive/?date=20050105&slug=healthasthma05m.

CHAPTER 1

Understanding Asthma

An Overview of Asthma

David A. Cramer, Teresa G. Odle, and Tish Davidson

In the selection that follows, three experts present an overview of a disease that affects millions worldwide. Asthma is a sometimes fatal condition of the lungs, characterized by inflammation of the tiny airways, that leads to severe difficulty in breathing. The authors cite the World Health Organization as estimating that 300 million people around the world suffer from asthma. That amounts to just under 5 percent of the global population. Rates in industrialized countries such as the United States are even higher, ranging between 5 and 10 percent. The disease often begins in childhood. Sometimes it diminishes or goes away altogether by adulthood, but in other individuals it remains for a lifetime. Still others develop the disease in middle age. Asthma cannot be cured, but treatments can help control it. One of the most important steps, say the authors, is to identify environmental triggers for asthma, which vary from person to person, and to encourage the patient to avoid them. David A. Cramer is program director and vice chair of emergency medicine at York Hospital in York, Pennsylvania. Teresa G. Odle and Tish Davidson are both nationally published medical writers.

Photo on previous page. Asthma sufferers have difficulty breathing, which is often evidenced by wheezing, coughing, and shortness of breath. (Coneyl Jay/ Photo Researchers, Inc.)

SOURCE: David A. Cramer, Teresa G. Odle, and Tish Davidson, "Asthma," *Gale Encyclopedia of Medicine,* 2007. Reproduced by permission of Gale, a part of Cengage Learning.

A sthma, also called hyperactive airway disease, is a recurrent inflammatory disease of the airways (breathing tubes). In individuals with asthma, the airways periodically spasm and narrow (a process called bronchoconstriction) in response to certain triggers. This makes breathing difficult, and the individual may wheeze, cough, and gasp for air. The airways relax and widen either spontaneously [or] in response [to] drug treatments.

Asthma is extremely common. The World Health Organization (WHO) estimates that in 2005, 300 million people worldwide were living with asthma and 255,000 people died of the disease. Asthma is the most common chronic disease among children. In 2007, between 5% and 10% of Americans experienced an asthma attack, including 5 million children. Over the past decade asthma among children younger than age 6 in industrialized countries appears to [be] increasing in both frequency and severity. In the United States asthma accounts for about 2 million emergency room visits annually, at least 500,000 hospitalizations, and 5,000 deaths.

A Complicated Malady

Asthma is a complex disease that involves at least five different kinds of white blood cells plus epithelial cells that line the airways. These cells release chemicals such as histamines and leukotrienes that trigger an inflammatory response and cause the epithelial cells to swell and secrete mucus. The changes that take place when these cells respond to an asthma trigger also cause the airways (*bronchi* and the smaller *bronchioles*) to narrow, making breathing difficult. Repeated exposure to asthma triggers (also called allergens) makes the airways hyperresponsive to stimuli that do not affect healthy lungs. An individual having an asthma attack often has as much or more difficulty exhaling as inhaling. Inability to exhale adequately can cause damage in the lung.

The Daily Toll of Asthma in America

Every day in America 40,000 people miss school or work, 5,000 people visit the emergency room, 1,000 people are admitted to the hospital, and 11 people die due to asthma.

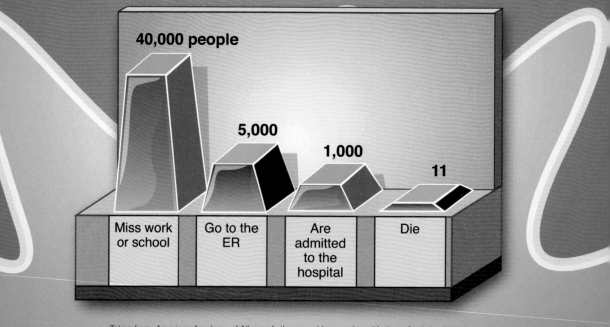

Taken from: American Academy of Allergy, Asthma, and Immunology, "Asthma Statistics," 2008. www.aaaai.org/media/resources/media_kit/asthma_statistics.stm.

Common triggers for asthma include:
- animal dander (the shed skin flakes from furry animals)
- aerosol sprays or chemical fumes
- cigarette smoke
- cold, dry air
- exercise
- fireplace smoke
- air pollution
- occupational exposure to chemicals, fumes, or particles of industrial materials in the air
- high pollen counts (trees, grasses, certain weeds)

- household dust (which includes a microscopic insect called a dust mite)
- cockroach allergens
- molds
- strong perfumes
- viral respiratory infections (common cold, influenza, RSV [respiratory syncytial virus])
- extreme stress or anxiety

Asthma in Children and Adults

Asthma can begin at any age, but most often begins in childhood or adolescence. About 20% of individuals with asthma have their first asthma attack before age one. When asthma begins in very early childhood, it often does so in a child who has a genetic predisposition to be hypersensitive to common allergens in the environment. This genetic sensitivity is called atopy, and it helps to explain why a tendency toward developing asthma runs in families. When atopic individuals are exposed to common allergens such as dust mites, animal dander, mold, pollen, cigarette smoke, or other potential allergens, they respond by producing antibodies that attempt to remove the allergens from the body. This makes the cells lining airways sensitive to the allergen. Repeat exposures rapidly produce an asthmatic response.

Many children wheeze when they have viral infections such as colds; not all of them have asthma. Fewer than half of children who have a wheezing episode before age three will have asthma at age six. Twice as many boys as girls have asthma until adolescence, when the rate evens out. Many children, especially boys, outgrow their asthma or have reduced responses in their late teens.

Asthma can develop at any age and in a wide variety of situations; however, most asthma cases that develop after age 40 are in women. Exposure to cigarette smoke, either through smoking or inhaling secondhand smoke, can trigger adult asthma, as can exposure to workplace chemicals, excessive amounts of dust, or air pollution. Asthma is highly individualized. Different people respond to different triggers, and the frequency and severity of response in the same individual can vary dramatically during their lifetime. Adults, however, are more likely to respond to stress as a trigger than are young children.

Causes and Symptoms

Most often asthma is caused by inhaling an allergen that sets off the chain of biochemical and tissue changes leading to airway swelling, bronchoconstriction, and difficulty breathing. Avoiding or minimizing exposure to allergens is the most effective way of managing asthma. Individuals respond to different allergens, so it is important to identify which allergen is causing symptoms in a particular individual. Once asthma is present, an attack can be triggered or worsened if the individual also has rhinitis (inflammation of the lining of the nose usually caused by a cold virus) or sinusitis (a sinus infection). Stomach acid passing back up the esophagus (acid reflux) can also trigger asthma or make it worse.

Asthma in some individuals may be triggered without exposure to allergens. In these cases, an asthma attack can be caused by sudden exposure to cold air, exercise, or high levels of stress and anxiety. Crying or even laughing may bring on an attack in some individuals.

The most obvious symptoms of asthma are wheezing and difficulty breathing. Wheezing is often loudest when the individual exhales. Besides wheezing and shortness of breath, the individual may cough and feel tightness in the chest. Children may have itching on their back or neck at the start of an attack.

Some individuals with asthma are free of symptoms most of the time but may occasionally be temporarily short of breath. People whose asthma is triggered by pollen often have seasonal symptoms. Some people have more or less continuous problems and their asthma is often worse at night. Severe episodes of asthma often occur when the individual gets a viral respiratory tract infection (a cold) or is exposed to a heavy load of an allergen or irritant, such as being in a room with smokers.

Shortness of breath may cause anxiety. To facilitate breathing the individual may sit upright, lean forward, and use the muscles of the neck and chest wall to help breathe. A person having an asthma attack may be able to say only a few words at a time before stopping to breathe.

Confusion and a bluish tint to the skin are clues that the oxygen supply is seriously low and emergency treatment is needed. In a severe attack that lasts for some time and does not respond to drug treatment (a condition called status asthmaticus), some of the tiny air sacs in the lung may rupture damaging the lung and making getting enough oxygen more difficult.

Asthma triggers an inflammatory response in the lungs that causes the lungs' bronchioles to constrict, making breathing difficult. (© Nucleus Medical Art, Inc./Alamy)

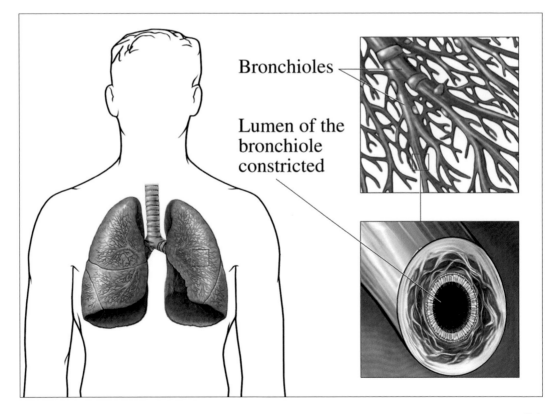

Bronchioles

Lumen of the bronchiole constricted

Diagnosing and Managing Asthma

Information about a family history of asthma or allergies can be a valuable indicator of asthma. Apart from listening to the individual's chest, the examiner should look for maximum chest expansion while taking in air. Hunched shoulders and contracted neck muscles are other signs of narrowed airways. Nasal polyps or increased amounts of nasal secretions are often noted in asthmatic individuals.

The diagnosis of asthma is strongly suggested when typical symptoms and signs are present. A pulmonary function test can then be performed with a device called a spirometer that measures how rapidly and completely air is exhaled from the lungs. Repeating spirometer measurements after the individual inhales a drug that widens the air passages (a bronchodilator) indicates whether the airway narrowing is reversible. Reversibility is a very typical finding in asthma. Often individuals use a related instrument, called a peak flow meter, to keep track of asthma severity when at home. . . .

An asthma attack should be treated immediately. Many people with asthma carry nebulizers [spray canisters] to inhale bronchodilators as needed during an attack. Children at schools with a zero tolerance for drugs may not be permitted to carry their nebulizer with them. Parents should check the school policy and determine if accommodations can be made for children who have severe asthma. Emergency medical care should be sought immediately in a severe attack or one that does not respond to inhaled medication. Asthma can be fatal. The individual may need supplemental oxygen or, rarely, mechanical ventilation to survive.

Educating both children and adults so that they can start treatment immediately once asthma is triggered

FAST FACT

The two main types of asthma medication are daily controllers and relievers. The daily controllers help prevent attacks, and the relievers ease symptoms when an attack occurs.

makes for minimal delay and helps the individual gain a sense of control over the disease. People with asthma should learn to monitor their symptoms so that they will be aware of when an attack is starting. People with asthma should also have a written "action plan" to follow if symptoms suddenly worsen, including how to adjust their medication and when to seek medical help.

The Causes of Asthma

USA Today Magazine

To identify the cause of a complex disease such as asthma is not an easy task. In the following selection *USA Today Magazine* explains the different causes behind asthma. According to the article, in order to control the occurrences of asthma attacks, one needs to familiarize oneself with common triggers such as allergies, environment, and exercise. *USA Today Magazine* is published by the Society for the Advancement of Education and addresses a variety of topics, including politics, ecology, and education, as they relate to U.S. national issues.

Asthma is caused by hyper-sensitive lungs that react to certain factors, or triggers. These vary widely among individuals afflicted with the condition. An important step in getting control of asthma is to identify and avoid the triggers that can cause attacks. According to the national pharmaceutical firm, Glaxo Inc., these include:

SOURCE: *USA Today Magazine*, "Identifying Attack Triggers," vol. 124, October 1995, p. 13. Copyright © 1995 Society for the Advancement of Education. Reproduced by permission.

The Role of Allergies

The lungs go into an episode or attack when the patient is in contact with things he or she is allergic to. Not everyone who has asthma is allergic, but a regular pattern or timing of symptoms often points to allergy as one cause. Seventy-five to 85% of asthma patients have positive reactions to common inhaled allergens, suggesting that allergy should be considered in diagnosis and treatment. Other allergic triggers include tiny particles, such as pollens and mold spores from trees, plants, and hay; animal dander, skin, hair, and feathers, including wool clothing and feather pillows; insects such as dust mites and cockroaches; foods such as nuts, chocolate, eggs, orange juice, fish, or milk; and chemical preservatives in foods and beverages.

Weather and Air Pollution as Triggers

Asthma symptoms tend to flare up with an assortment of weather conditions, including rapid changes in temperature and barometric pressure. High humidity favors

This drawing shows a normal bronchus in the lungs and one that is inflamed with asthma and secreting mucus. (© Nucleus Medical Art, Inc./Alamy)

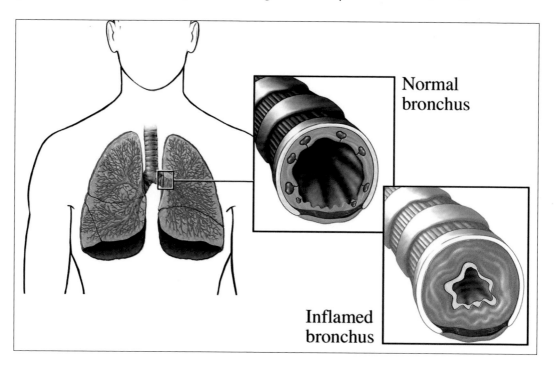

Normal bronchus

Inflamed bronchus

mold growth; windy days increase airborne pollen; and, in winter, cold air can cause bronchial muscles to constrict, making breathing difficult. Certain weather patterns such as inversions and air stagnation can cause a build-up of industrial air pollution. Common weather/air pollution triggers include pollens and molds, affected by weather patterns; summer heat; cold dry winter air; industrial smokestacks, automobiles, and trucks; cigarette smoke; dirt, gases, vapors, and smoke; and traffic jams, parking garages, dusty work areas, and smoke-filled rooms.

Exercise and Exertion

Symptoms occur because of a loss of heat or water, or both, from the lungs during exercise. Most asthmatics have airway hyper-irritability that leads to exercise-induced asthma (EIA). Although individual episodes of EIA are short-lived, their severity and impact can be striking; as a result, people with untreated EIA often limit their activities unnecessarily. Use of a pretreatment regimen usually allows normal participation in activities.

One common myth about asthma is that only heavy exercise can cause an attack; actually, simple exertion also is a common trigger. For many sufferers, simply going up stairs, carrying groceries, or walking the dog can cause an attack.

Occupational Triggers

One's job environment can result in exposure to irritants as well as allergens. The connection between the work environment and asthma symptoms is complicated by delayed reactions, which often occur several hours after exposure. Occupational triggers include wood and organic dusts; metals, gases, and aerosols; raw cotton, flax, hemp dust, and mold; ammonia, hydrochloric acid, chlorine, and

> **FAST FACT**
>
> Practitioners of traditional Chinese healing believe that "wheezy breathing" (which we know as asthma) is caused by an imbalance of qi, a supposed vital force in the body. They treat it with acupuncture and herbal remedies.

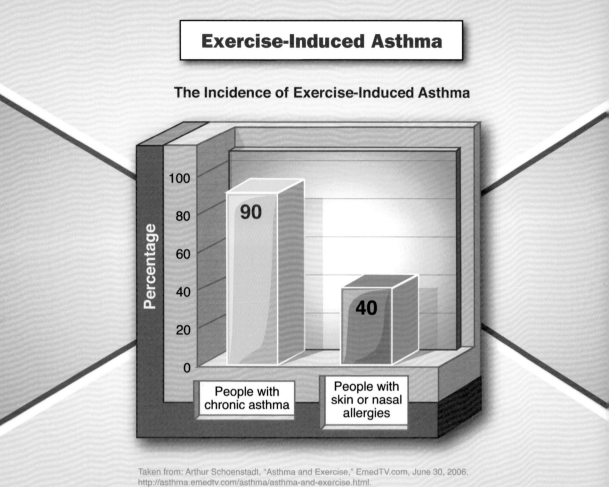

Exercise-Induced Asthma

The Incidence of Exercise-Induced Asthma

Percentage

- 100
- 80
- 60
- 40
- 20
- 0

90 — People with chronic asthma

40 — People with skin or nasal allergies

Taken from: Arthur Schoenstadt, "Asthma and Exercise," EmedTV.com, June 30, 2006.
http://asthma.emedtv.com/asthma/asthma-and-exercise.html.

sulfur dioxide; flour; soldering fluxes; henna; and poly-vinylchloride (PVC) products.

Emotional Effects

Asthma is not "all in one's head," but strong emotions can affect a patient's breathing and trigger an attack. Laughing, crying, or yelling can stimulate nerves that cause muscles in the airways to tighten, leading to an exacerbation of the condition. Fear and anxiety can occur during an episode and may cause a patient to breathe too hard and fast—worsening the attack. Anger or frustration with the disease may cause a patient to refuse to take the medicines needed to prevent attacks.

The Diagnosis of Asthma

Cleveland Clinic

Asthma is a particularly difficult condition to diagnose. In the following selection specialists at the Cleveland Clinic describe various techniques used to determine whether a patient is suffering from the disease. These techniques include various kinds of pulmonary (lung) function tests. They range from a simple test of the lungs' maximum capacity and power to a test that tries to trigger an asthma attack by introducing the substance methacholine into the lungs to see if they react. In addition to pulmonary tests, doctors may image the lungs and airways to see what is going on inside. Sophisticated X-ray equipment may be used to produce what is known as a CT (computerized tomography) scan. Lastly, doctors will try to uncover related conditions, such as sinus infections, that could complicate the treatment of asthma. The Cleveland Clinic is a not-for-profit academic medical center that integrates clinical and hospital care with research and education. Based in Cleveland, Ohio, it has branches throughout that state and satellite clinics in various other states and countries. It was founded in 1921 by four renowned physicians.

SOURCE: Cleveland Clinic, "Diagnosing Asthma," December 14, 2006. my.clevelandclinic.org. Reproduced by permission.

To diagnose asthma, your doctor will review your medical history, family history, and symptoms. He or she will be interested in any history of breathing problems you might have had, as well as a family history of asthma or other lung conditions, allergies, or a skin disease called eczema. It is important that you describe your symptoms in detail (coughing, wheezing, shortness of breath, chest tightness), including when and how often they occur.

Your doctor will also perform a physical examination and listen to your heart and lungs.

There are many tests your doctor might perform, including pulmonary function tests, allergy tests, blood tests, and chest and sinus X-rays. All of these tests help your doctor determine if asthma is indeed present and if there are other conditions affecting it.

Types of Lung Tests

Pulmonary function tests (or lung function tests) include numerous procedures to diagnose lung problems. The two most common lung function tests used to diagnose asthma are spirometry and methacholine challenge tests.

Spirometry. This is a simple breathing test that measures how much and how fast you can blow air out of your lungs. It is often used to determine the amount of airway obstruction you have. Spirometry can be done before and after you inhale a short-acting medication called a bronchodilator, such as albuterol. The bronchodilator causes your airways to expand, allowing for air to pass through freely. This test might also be done at future doctor visits to monitor your progress and help your doctor determine if and how to adjust your treatment plan.

Methacholine Challenge Test. This test is more commonly used in adults than children. It might be performed if your symptoms and screening spirometry do not clearly or convincingly establish a diagnosis of asthma. Methacholine is an agent that, when inhaled, causes the airways

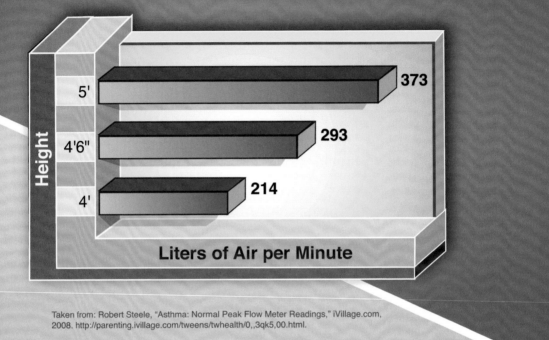

Normal Peak Flow Rates for Children

The peak expiratory flow rate measures how fast a person can exhale air. It is one of a number of tests that measure how efficiently your airways work.

Height

5'	373
4'6"	293
4'	214

Liters of Air per Minute

Taken from: Robert Steele, "Asthma: Normal Peak Flow Meter Readings," iVillage.com, 2008. http://parenting.ivillage.com/tweens/twhealth/0,,3qk5,00.html.

to spasm and narrow if asthma is present. During this test, you inhale increasing amounts of methacholine aerosol mist before and after spirometry. The methacholine test is considered positive—meaning asthma is present—if the lung function drops by at least 20 percent. A bronchodilator is always administered at the end of the test to reverse the effects of the methacholine.

Ask your doctor if there is anything you need to do to prepare for spirometry.

Before taking a methacholine challenge test, be sure to tell your doctor if you have recently had a viral infection, like a cold, or any shots or immunizations, since these might affect the test's results.

Other general preparations to follow before the test include:

- No smoking on the day of the test
- No coffee, tea, cola, or chocolate on the day of test
- Avoid exercise and cold air exposure on the day of test

Medicines taken to treat asthma can affect the test results. Different medicines must be stopped at different intervals. For example, short-acting inhaled bronchodilators should be stopped eight hours before testing, but long-acting inhaled bronchodilators cannot be taken for 48 hours. Your doctor will tell you how long before testing you should discontinue any medicines you are taking.

An X-ray Diagnosis

An X-ray is an image of the body that is created by using low doses of radiation reflected on special film or a fluorescent screen. X-rays can be used to diagnose a wide range of conditions, from bronchitis to a broken bone. Your doctor might perform an X-ray exam on you in order to see the structures inside your chest, including the heart, lungs, and bones. By viewing your lungs, your doctor can see if asthma is causing your symptoms.

There are some medical conditions that might make asthma harder to treat and control. Two of these conditions are sinusitis and gastroesophageal reflux disease, commonly called GERD. If you are diagnosed with asthma, your doctor might also test you for these conditions so that they can be treated.

Sinusitis, also called sinus infection, is an inflammation or swelling of the sinuses due to infection. When the sinuses become blocked and filled with

FAST FACT

Asthma is not the only condition that produces symptoms of wheezing and difficulty in breathing. Other lung diseases such as chronic obstructive pulmonary disease (COPD), bronchitis, or pneumonia could be responsible.

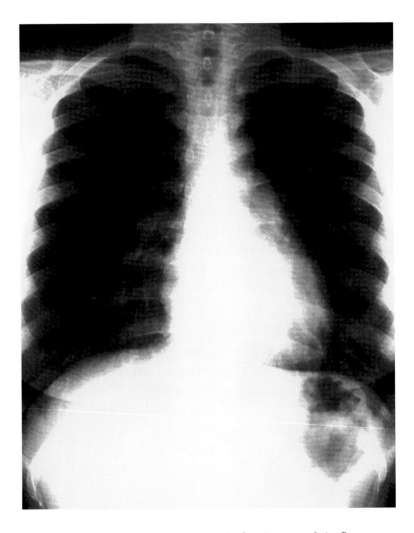

A digitally colored X-ray showing a normal human chest. (© Mike Hill/Alamy)

fluid, bacteria grow, causing infection and inflammation. Your doctor might order a special X-ray, called a CT [computerized tomography] scan, to evaluate your sinuses if he or she suspects an infection. Once acute sinusitis is diagnosed, you will be treated with antibiotics for at least 10 to 12 days.

The Treatment of Asthma

National Heart, Lung, and Blood Institute

The treatment of a chronic, or long-running, disease requires a lot of involvement by the patient. In the following selection the National Heart, Lung, and Blood Institute explains the treatment protocols and how a person with asthma can best manage his or her disease. Successful treatment, the institute suggests, requires a well-informed partnership between patient and physician. The first step is to identify what environmental factors trigger an attack. It might be cigarette smoke, an allergic reaction to pollen, a food sensitivity, or even just exercise. Once triggers have been identified, it is up to the patient to be careful to avoid them. Doctors will typically prescribe two kinds of medicine to help in the treatment of asthma. One is for daily use to help reduce the inflammation that leads to an attack. The other is for quick relief in case an attack occurs. Asthma cannot be cured, the selection states, but successful management can reduce the frequency of attacks and even the amount of medicine required to prevent them. The National Heart, Lung, and Blood Institute is a component of the National Institutes of Health, a federally operated organization dedicated to advancing public health through research and education.

SOURCE: National Heart, Lung, and Blood Institute, "How Is Asthma Treated and Controlled?" September 2008. nhlbi.nih.gov.

Asthma is a long-term disease that can't be cured. The goal of asthma treatment is to control the disease. . . .

To reach this goal, you should actively partner with your doctor to manage your asthma or your child's asthma. Children aged 10 or older—and younger children who are able—also should take an active role in their asthma care.

Taking an active role to control your asthma involves working with your doctor and other clinicians on your health care team to create and follow an asthma action plan. It also means avoiding factors that can make your asthma flare up and treating other conditions that can interfere with asthma management.

An asthma action plan gives guidance on taking your medicines properly, avoiding factors that worsen your asthma, tracking your level of asthma control, responding to worsening asthma, and seeking emergency care when needed.

Drug Interventions

Asthma is treated with two types of medicines: long-term control and quick-relief medicines. Long-term control medicines help reduce airway inflammation and prevent asthma symptoms. Quick-relief, or "rescue," medicines relieve asthma symptoms that may flare up.

Your initial asthma treatment will depend on how severe your disease is. Followup asthma treatment will depend on how well your asthma action plan is working to control your symptoms and prevent you from having asthma attacks.

Your level of asthma control can vary over time and with changes in your home, school, or work environments that alter how often you are exposed to the factors that can make your asthma worse. Your doctor may need to increase your medicine if your asthma doesn't stay under control.

On the other hand, if your asthma is well controlled for several months, your doctor may be able to decrease your medicine. These adjustments either up or down to your medicine will help you maintain the best control possible with the least amount of medicine necessary.

Asthma treatment for certain groups of people, such as children, pregnant women, or those for whom exercise brings on asthma symptoms, will need to be adjusted to meet their special needs. . . .

Avoiding Hazards Can Prevent Complications

A number of common things (sometimes called asthma triggers) can set off or worsen your asthma symptoms. Once you know what these factors are, you can take steps to control many of them.

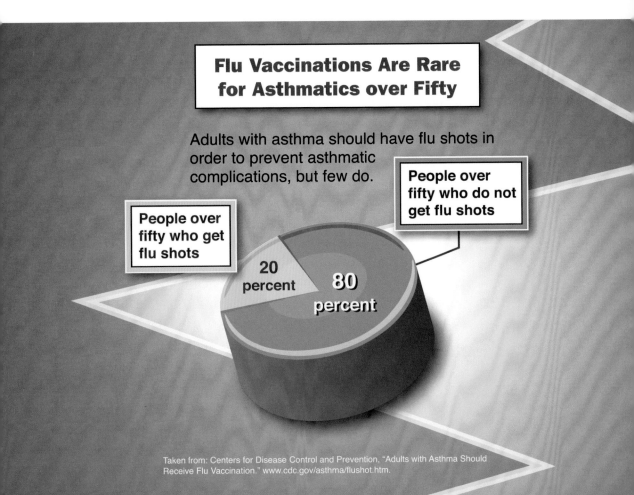

Flu Vaccinations Are Rare for Asthmatics over Fifty

Adults with asthma should have flu shots in order to prevent asthmatic complications, but few do.

People over fifty who get flu shots

People over fifty who do not get flu shots

20 percent

80 percent

Taken from: Centers for Disease Control and Prevention, "Adults with Asthma Should Receive Flu Vaccination." www.cdc.gov/asthma/flushot.htm.

For example, if exposure to pollens or air pollution makes your asthma worse, try to limit time outdoors when the levels of these substances are high in the outdoor air. If animal fur sets off your asthma symptoms, keep pets with fur out of your home or bedroom. . . .

If your asthma symptoms are clearly linked to allergies, and you can't avoid exposure to those allergens, then your doctor may advise you to get allergy shots for the specific allergens that bother your asthma. You may need to see a specialist if you're thinking about getting allergy shots. These shots may lessen or prevent your asthma symptoms, but they can't cure your asthma.

Several health conditions can make asthma more difficult to manage. These conditions include runny nose, sinus infections, reflux disease, psychological stress, and sleep apnea. . . .

The Use of Inhalers

Asthma medicines can be taken in pill form, but most are taken using a device called an inhaler. An inhaler allows the medicine to go right to your lungs.

Not all inhalers are used the same way. Ask your doctor and other clinicians on your health care team to show you the right way to use your inhaler. Ask them to review the way you use your inhaler at every visit.

Most people who have asthma need to take long-term control medicines daily to help prevent symptoms. The most effective long-term medicines reduce airway inflammation. These medicines are taken over the long term to prevent symptoms from starting. They don't give you quick relief from symptoms.

Inhaled corticosteroids are the preferred medicines for long-term control of asthma. These medicines are the most effective long-term control medicine to relieve airway inflammation and swelling that makes the airways sensitive to certain substances that are breathed in.

Reducing inflammation helps prevent the chain reaction that causes asthma symptoms. Most people who take these medicines daily find they greatly reduce how severe symptoms are and how often they occur.

Side Effects Can Be Avoided

Inhaled corticosteroids are generally safe when taken as prescribed. They're very different from the illegal anabolic steroids taken by some athletes. Inhaled corticosteroids aren't habit-forming, even if you take them every day for many years.

But, like many other medicines, inhaled corticosteroids can have side effects. Most doctors agree that the benefits of taking inhaled corticosteroids and preventing asthma attacks far outweigh the risks of side effects.

One common side effect from inhaled corticosteroids is a mouth infection called thrush. You can use a spacer or holding chamber to avoid thrush. A spacer or holding chamber is attached to your inhaler when taking medicine to keep the medicine from landing in your mouth or on the back of your throat. . . .

If you have severe asthma, you may have to take corticosteroid pills or liquid for short periods to get your asthma under control. If taken for long periods, these medicines raise your risk for cataracts and osteoporosis. A cataract is the clouding of the lens in your eye. Osteoporosis is a disorder that makes your bones weak and more likely to break.

Your doctor may have you add another long-term control asthma medicine to lower your dose of corticosteroids. Or, your doctor may suggest you take calcium and vitamin D pills to protect your bones. . . .

FAST FACT

A new generation of asthma medicines in the form of pills or powders reduces inflammation with less risk of mouth infection.

Most asthma sufferers use a device called an inhaler, which allows medication to be directly administered to the lungs. (© Bubbles Photolibrary/Alamy)

The Rapid Response Medicine

All people who have asthma need a quick-relief medicine to help relieve asthma symptoms that may flare up. Inhaled short-acting beta$_2$-agonists are the first choice for quick relief.

These medicines act quickly to relax tight muscles around your airways when you're having a flareup. This allows the airways to open up so air can flow through them.

You should take your quick-relief medicine when you first notice your asthma symptoms. If you use this medicine more than 2 days a week, talk with your doctor about how well controlled your asthma is. You may need to make changes in your asthma action plan.

Carry your quick-relief inhaler with you at all times in case you need it. If your child has asthma, make sure that anyone caring for him or her and the child's school has the child's quick-relief medicines. They should understand when and how to use them and when to seek medical care for your child. . . .

Measuring Air Flow

[A] small, hand-held device [known as a peak flow meter] shows how well air moves out of your lungs. You blow into the device and it gives you a score, or peak flow number. Your score shows how well your lungs are working at the time of the test.

Your doctor will tell you how and when to use your peak flow meter. He or she also will teach you how to take your medicines based on your score.

Your doctor and other clinicians on your health care team may ask you to use your peak flow meter each morning and keep a record of your results. It may be particularly useful to record peak flow scores for a couple of weeks before each medical visit and take the results with you.

When first diagnosed with asthma, it's important to find out your "personal best" peak flow number. To do this, you record your score each day for a 2- to 3-week period when your asthma is under good control. The highest number you get during that time is your personal best. You can compare this number to future numbers to make sure your asthma is under control.

Your peak flow meter can help warn you of an asthma attack, even before you notice symptoms. If your score falls to a number that shows that your breathing is getting worse, you should take your quick-relief medicines the way your asthma action plan directs. Then you can use the peak flow meter to check how well the medicine worked.

Asthma Checkups Should Be Regular

When you first begin treatment, you will see your doctor about every 2 to 6 weeks. Once your asthma is under control, your doctor may want to see you anywhere from once a month to twice a year.

During these checkups, your doctor or nurse will ask whether you've had an asthma attack since the last visit or any changes in symptoms or peak flow measurements. You will also be asked about your daily activities. This will help them assess your level of asthma control.

Your doctor or nurse also will ask whether you have any problems or concerns with taking your medicines or following your asthma action plan. Based on your answers to these questions, your doctor may change the dose of your medicine or give you a new medicine.

If your control is very good, you may be able to take less medicine. The goal is to use the least amount of medicine needed to control your asthma.

Self-Care for Asthmatics

Carl Sherman

In the following selection Carl Sherman argues that a more active role for asthma patients can lead to better control of their condition. Sherman says that by having asthma patients take home measurements of lung function over a period of time, doctors can determine the severity of the disease better than just relying on numbers from lab tests. The patients can also use the home monitoring to adjust their medication or seek assistance if needed. These changes in the treatment of asthma result from the realization that the severity of asthma can change over time, thus requiring treatment to change as well, Sherman says. Sherman is a medical writer from New York City.

S ince 1993, the Global Initiative for Asthma (GINA) has issued periodic treatment guidelines, with yearly updates to incorporate new research findings. The most recent *Global Strategy for Asthma Management and Prevention*, which was released in November 2006, represents a major revision that embodies a fundamental

SOURCE: Carl Sherman, "Symptom Control: New Approach Is Key to Managing Asthma," *Cortlandt Forum*, February 10, 2007. Copyright © 2007 Haymarket Media, Inc. Reproduced by permission.

When asthma patients take regular measurements of their lung function at home, doctors are better able to determine the effectiveness of treatment. (© Scott Camazine/Alamy)

change in approach: While earlier versions recommended treatment on the basis of asthma severity—intermittent and mild, moderate, and severe persistent—the latest revision emphasizes degree of control.

The change comes out of a recognition that severity may change over time and that a more clinically relevant stratification takes into account both underlying disease and responsiveness to treatment.

"Is the patient sleeping through the night? Has he had to use his rescue inhaler every day? Is he able to carry out the activities of daily life? Based on the patient's responses, the doctor will step up treatment, leave it unchanged, or step it down. This approach is more consistent with how primary-care physicians actually practice," comments Jeffrey M. Drazen, MD, professor of medicine at Harvard Medical School in Boston, editor-in-chief of *The New England Journal of Medicine,* and a member of the GINA science committee that wrote the guidelines.

A New Approach

This focus on severity, according to the guidelines' authors, is emphasized throughout the new document and reflects pharmacologic advances that have made essentially normal lives a reasonable expectation for the vast majority of patients coping with asthma.

The guidelines define full control as:

- Daytime symptoms no more than twice a week
- No limitations of daily activities, including exercise
- No nocturnal symptoms or awakenings
- Reliever treatment needed no more than twice a week
- Normal or near-normal lung function tests
- No exacerbations

Within this model, management is presented as a dynamic process in which assessment guides treatment and control is monitored in a continuous cycle. The guidelines stress that increased use of reliever (rescue) medications (especially on a daily basis) is a warning of deteriorating control.

Assessment

As earlier, assessment of lung function by spirometry and peak expiratory flow is a keystone of diagnosis and monitoring. New prominence, however, is given to variability in these parameters, determined by a history that may rely to some extent on home measurement. "A number in the lab is not as sensitive as change over time," Dr. Drazen observes.

The degree to which measures of lung function fluctuate in the course of a day, from month to month, or from season to season is now regarded as an important index of disease severity and control that plays an important role in clinical decisions and in determining the need for further investigation, such as airway-responsiveness testing.

FAST FACT

Some personal asthma plans relate the peak flow meter readings to a traffic light: 80 percent of one's personal best is a green light for go, 50 to 80 percent is a yellow light for caution, and 50 percent or below means stop and get help.

An Active Partnership

The 2006 revision gives new prominence to development of the patient/doctor partnership, treating it as a major component of management along with reducing exposure to risk factors and the step-based assessment-treatment-monitoring cycle. The aim of the partnership is a program of "guided self-management" through which patients can control their own condition under professional supervision.

The guidelines emphasize education to prepare patients with asthma for their more active role: This includes information on various medications and training

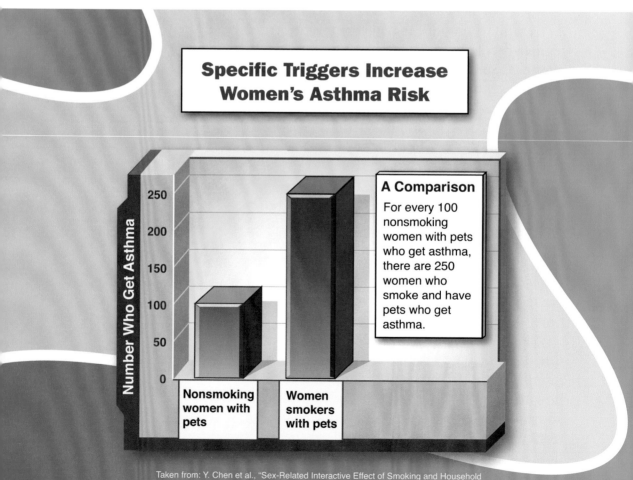

Specific Triggers Increase Women's Asthma Risk

A Comparison

For every 100 nonsmoking women with pets who get asthma, there are 250 women who smoke and have pets who get asthma.

Number Who Get Asthma

Nonsmoking women with pets

Women smokers with pets

Taken from: Y. Chen et al., "Sex-Related Interactive Effect of Smoking and Household Pets on Asthma Incidence," *European Respiratory Journal*, vol. 20, 2002, p. 1162.

in their use as well as strategies for preventing symptoms and attacks. Patients participate in the development of a written action plan and help execute it by monitoring their own lung function and symptoms, adjusting medication when necessary, and seeking appropriate medical assistance.

The guidelines recognize that asthma management is chiefly the province of primary-care physicians. "But referral is indicated if the patient has to be on two controller medications and asthma is still not in excellent control," Dr. Drazen says.

Drug Choices

Pharmacotherapy is set forth in steps that are largely defined by the type, dosage, and number of controller medications needed. Within the step schema, the guidelines set forth preferred and other drug options.

The Burden of Childhood Asthma

A. Ursulla Courtney, Daniel F. McCarter, and Susan M. Pollart

Asthma is increasingly common as a childhood disease. In the following selection three family doctors describe the development and treatment of asthma in children. Allergies play a significant role in the onset of asthma, they say. The type of allergy ranges widely, from food sensitivities to allergic skin rash to nasal allergies. Allergies lead to inflammation, which is a key factor in asthma. The authors state that the early treatment of allergies with antihistamines (drugs that help suppress inflammation) or other therapies may head off asthma before it develops. Once a child has asthma, the course of treatment differs somewhat from that for adults. The benefits and side effects of certain drug treatments differ, the authors indicate. For example, some drugs retard a child's growth rate, whereas an adult already has full height. However, children benefit from an effort to keep asthma triggers, such as allergens or cigarette smoke, out of their living environment, just as adults do. A. Ursulla Courtney is a family medicine physician in the University of Virginia Health System. Daniel F. McCarter and Susan M. Pollart are doctors in family practice in Charlottesville, Virginia.

SOURCE: A. Ursulla Courtney, Daniel F. McCarter, and Susan M. Pollart, "Childhood Asthma: Treatment Update," *American Family Physician,* May 15, 2005. Copyright © 2005 American Academy of Family Physicians. Reprinted with permission.

Asthma is a chronic lung disease characterized by recurrent cough and wheeze that is increasing in prevalence among children. More than 5 percent of the U.S. population younger than 18 years—nearly 5 million children—is affected by this disorder. It is found more often in patients with a personal or family history of atopy [genetic predisposition to allergies]. . . .

The development of asthma in children is thought to be the final step in a disease process described as the "allergic march." The allergic march may begin in infancy with food allergy–associated gastrointestinal disorders and dermatitis [skin inflammation]. Allergic rhinoconjunctivitis [nose and eye inflammation] follows in early childhood, and asthma often completes the picture. . . . Recent data from randomized controlled trials (RCTs) have suggested that early use of some antihistamines or immunotherapy may reduce the number of children who progress from rhinoconjunctivitis to asthma.

Asthma causes airway hyperresponsiveness, airflow limitation, and persistent respiratory symptoms such as wheezing, coughing, chest tightness, and shortness of breath. The majority of children with asthma develop symptoms before five years of age. Because the symptoms vary extensively, asthma must be distinguished from other causes of respiratory illness. Demonstrating reversible airway obstruction in children old enough to perform peak flow measurements or spirometry provides an objective means of confirming the diagnosis. Once a child is diagnosed with asthma, the goal of therapy is to reduce wheeze and cough, reduce the risk and number of acute exacerbations, and minimize adverse effects of treatments, sleep disturbances, and absences from school. Treatment is tailored to the severity of asthma. . . .

Treatment During Attacks

Beta$_2$ Agonists. In an acute asthma exacerbation, inhaled beta$_2$ agonists are a mainstay of treatment. Administration of an inhaled beta$_2$ agonist via a metered-dose inhaler with a spacer device is equally as effective as nebulized therapy. There is no evidence to support the use of oral or intravenous beta$_2$ agonists in the treatment of acute asthma. There is some evidence that high-dose nebulized beta$_2$ agonists administered every 20 minutes for six doses may be more effective than low-dose beta$_2$ agonists in treating severe acute asthma in children. . . .

Supplemental Oxygen. Despite the absence of RCT data, it is common practice to use supplemental oxygen in children with acute asthma exacerbations treated in the emergency department. Low oxygen saturation measured with pulse oximetry has been correlated inversely with the rate of hospitalization. However, poor sensitivity and

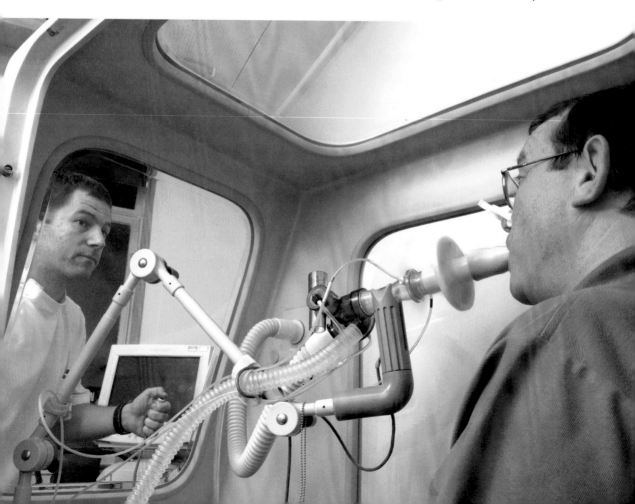

A doctor uses a spirometer to perform a lung function test on a patient, a means of detecting asthma and other lung disorders. (Tim Vernon/ LTH NHS Trust/Photo Researchers, Inc.)

specificity limit the use of oxygen saturation as a single indicator to determine the need for hospitalization.

Anticholinergics. The addition of inhaled ipratropium bromide (Atrovent) to each inhalation of a beta$_2$ agonist is more effective than the beta$_2$ agonist alone in children with an acute asthma exacerbation. A systematic review of the evidence showed that one hospitalization is prevented for every 12 children treated with this therapy and one for every seven children with a severe exacerbation.

Corticosteroids. Oral corticosteroids given early during an acute asthma exacerbation (i.e., within 45 minutes of the onset of symptoms) reduce the likelihood of hospital admission. In addition, oral corticosteroids are more effective than inhaled or nebulized corticosteroids in children hospitalized with severe acute asthma. Repeated short courses of oral corticosteroids, at a dose of 1 mg per kg per day, in the treatment of acute flares of asthma do not appear to cause any lasting changes in bone metabolism, bone mineralization, or adrenal function. There is no evidence that intravenous corticosteroids are any more effective than oral corticosteroids in children with an intact and functioning digestive tract.

A systematic review of additional studies in the emergency department—including three pediatric studies—demonstrated that inhaled corticosteroids in high doses reduce hospital admission rates in patients with acute asthma. However, there is insufficient evidence that inhaled corticosteroids alone are as effective as systemic steroids. . . .

Long-Term Therapies

Corticosteroids. Inhaled corticosteroids are a standard part of maintenance therapy for asthma. Studies have shown that, as a single agent, inhaled corticosteroids in a medium dosage are more effective than inhaled long-acting beta$_2$ agonists, inhaled nedocromil (Tilade), and leukotriene inhibitors in improving asthma symptoms and lung function in children with mild to moderate asthma. There also is less use of bronchodilators and oral corticosteroids in patients using maintenance inhaled corticosteroids. Some short-term studies have found [a] reduced [rate of] growth in children using inhaled corticosteroids regularly. However, multiple studies have found no evidence that children treated with inhaled corticosteroids fail to reach their full adult height.

Unlike adults, children whose asthma is inadequately controlled with standard dosages of inhaled corticosteroids have not been shown to benefit from the addition of a long-acting beta$_2$ agonist or from an increase in the dosage of inhaled corticosteroids. In two RCTs, benefit was demonstrated at three months with the addition of long-acting beta$_2$ agonists, but 12-month follow-up in one of these studies found no difference in objective measures of lung function, symptom scores, or exacerbation rate. . . .

Oral Theophylline. Oral theophylline initially seemed promising in the prophylactic treatment of childhood asthma. When compared with placebo, it significantly increased the mean morning peak expiratory flow rate and reduced the mean number of acute nighttime attacks and doses of bronchodilator used. However, it proved to be less promising when its use over one year was compared with the use of inhaled corticosteroids. Although there was no significant difference between theophylline and inhaled corticosteroids in reduction of asthma symptoms, there was an increased use of short-acting beta$_2$ agonists and oral corticosteroids in children receiving theophylline. In summary, its use in children cannot be recommended because of the potential for serious side effects, such as cardiac arrhythmias or convulsions, if therapeutic blood levels are exceeded.

Immunotherapy. Immunotherapy can be used as an adjunct to standard drug therapy in allergic asthmatic children. Sublingual (allergy drops) and injectable (aller-

Children Need Emergency Treatment for Asthma More Often than Adults

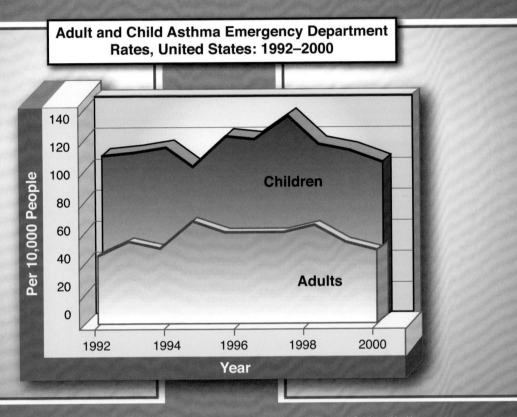

Adult and Child Asthma Emergency Department Rates, United States: 1992–2000

Taken from: Seymour Williams, "Asthma in U.S. Children: Update," National Business Group on Health, April 11, 2008. Data from National Hospital Ambulatory Care Survey, National Center for Health Statistics.

gy shots) therapies have been shown to reduce the presence of asthma and the overall use of asthma medication. Standard immunotherapy has a 1.7 to 15 percent reported range of adverse effects, but between 1985 and 1989, there were 17 standard immunotherapy-related deaths reported in the United States.

Strategies for Self-Help

Education. Educating parents and caregivers of children with asthma to recognize and avoid triggers, and to understand the use of prescribed medications, the proper use of inhalation devices, and the importance of compliance and monitoring, has been shown to improve lung function and decrease school absenteeism and visits to the emergency department. Educational programs for the self-management of asthma by children and adolescents have similar outcomes. Children with moderate to severe asthma receive the most benefit from educational programs. The relative effectiveness of the various components of these programs has not been compared directly. However, education for children who have received emergency department care for asthma does not reduce subsequent emergency department care, hospitalizations, or unscheduled doctor visits.

Reducing Asthma Triggers. Asthma triggers include allergens (i.e., dust, mites, pollen), irritants (i.e., smoke, perfumes), physical environment (i.e., exercise, cold air), physiologic triggers (i.e., viral infections), and pharmacologic therapies (i.e., beta blockers). Environmental controls such as removal of carpeting in the child's bedroom, and the use of pillow and mattress covers and air filtration systems have been suggested as ways to reduce asthma symptoms. However, recent evidence from better quality studies has shown that dust-mite avoidance measures (using impermeable mattress and pillow covers) did not improve symptoms or reduce medication use in adults with moderate to severe asthma. A similar study of children with allergic rhinitis showed no improvement in rhinitis symptoms using impermeable mattress and pillow covers compared with conventional covers. The role of avoidance measures as an adjunct to pharmacotherapy or immunotherapy has not been well studied. There is insufficient evidence to recommend for or against the use of air filtration units to reduce allergen levels in an effort to improve asthma symptoms. . . .

FAST FACT

Emotional stress such as anxiety, frustration, or anger can trigger asthma in children, but only if the asthmatic condition is already present. By 2006 the number of American children with asthma had risen to an estimated 6.8 million, with some 1.2 million under age five.

A Promising New Drug

Several new therapies have been introduced for the treatment of allergic asthma in children. . . . Omalizumab is approved for use in children 12 years and older with moderate to severe persistent asthma who have a positive skin test or in vitro reactivity to a perennial aeroallergen and whose symptoms are inadequately controlled with inhaled corticosteroids. In children with moderate to severe asthma, omalizumab reduces the rate of serious asthma exacerbations and the need for physician or emergency department visits and hospitalizations, and improves asthma quality-of-life scores. Although this new agent seems promising, its use is likely to be limited because it has an estimated cost of $10,000 per patient per year. Its use may be cost-effective if limited to allergic asthmatics who are poorly controlled on maximal therapy and who are hospitalized five or more times (or for 20 days or longer) per year.

Asthma and Exercise

Arthur Schoenstadt

Exercise is generally considered a positive factor for health. For people who suffer from asthma, however, exercise can bring on an attack. In the following selection physician Arthur Schoenstadt explains how asthma patients can lessen the chances of exercise-induced asthma and still lead an active life. Asthmatic patients who suffer from skin allergies or hay fever often overlap with those who experience exercise-induced asthma. Among the key steps, he says, are to avoid exercising in cold air or outdoors when there is a lot of pollen in the air. Additionally, certain sports seem more prone to trigger asthma than others; these sports, such as cycling and hockey, are generally characterized by high intensity or being set in cold, dry air. An attractive sport for someone with asthma is swimming (because it takes place in warm, moist air), Schoenstadt notes. But he adds that for older adults swimming does not provide all the benefits for bone health found in exercises that force the body to work against gravity. Schoenstadt is a physician based in Issaquah, Washington.

While there is a link between asthma and exercise, just because a person has asthma, it doesn't mean he or she can't participate in sports or other forms of exercise. Some sports (such as basketball) are more likely to trigger asthma symptoms than others. Statistics on asthma and exercise indicate that exercise-induced asthma occurs in almost 40 percent of individuals who have allergic rhinitis or atopic dermatitis.

Exercise-induced asthma is the development of asthma symptoms during exercise. Exercise-induced asthma

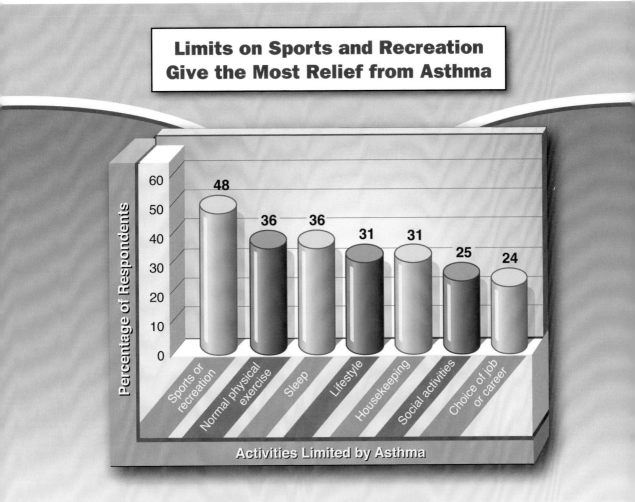

Limits on Sports and Recreation Give the Most Relief from Asthma

Percentage of Respondents

Activities Limited by Asthma

Sports or recreation: 48
Normal physical exercise: 36
Sleep: 36
Lifestyle: 31
Housekeeping: 31
Social activities: 25
Choice of job or career: 24

Taken from: Cipla Doc, *Foracort Forum*, no.1, Cipladoc.com, 2000.
www.cipladoc.com/publications/Respiratory/Publication/foracort/foracortissue01.htm.

triggers the airways to become narrower, and less air flows through to your lung tissues. For those with exercise-induced asthma, it can be hard to exercise for more than 30 minutes at a time. Exercise-induced asthma symptoms typically start after 5 to 20 minutes of nonstop exercise, and may include cough, wheezing, difficulty breathing, and/or chest tightness.

FAST FACT

Exercise-induced asthma is more common in those who suffer from poor physical condition or respiratory infections.

Everyone Needs Exercise

Regular physical exercise is important for good health. If exercise brings on asthma symptoms, work with your doctor to find the best way to avoid having symptoms when you exercise.

Some people with asthma use inhaled quick-relief medication before exercising to keep their symptoms under control. If you use your asthma medication as directed and learn how to pace yourself, you should be able to take part in any physical activity or sport you choose. In fact, many Olympic athletes have asthma.

Warming up and cooling down for at least 15 minutes before and after exercise may help lessen your symptoms. Avoiding exercise in extremely cold temperatures or when pollen levels are high may also help reduce your symptoms.

Sports Pose Varying Risks

Certain sports seem to be more likely to trigger an asthma attack, including sports associated with cool, dry air and high-intensity sports. Sports more likely to induce an asthma attack include the following:

- Basketball
- Soccer
- Cycling
- Long-distance running
- Hockey
- Cross-country skiing
- Speed skating

Other sports that are less likely to trigger an asthma attack include moderate-intensity activities, such as baseball, football, tennis, volleyball, and wrestling.

People with asthma who want to remain physically active often choose swimming because it is the least likely activity to trigger an asthma attack.

Keep in mind that for older adults, swimming does not have the same beneficial impact on bone health as weight-bearing exercises that work the body against gravity, such as the following activities:

- Walking
- Jogging
- Racquet sports
- Basketball
- Volleyball
- Aerobics
- Dancing
- Weight training

Physically active people with asthma often choose swimming as the least likely sports activity to trigger an asthma attack.
(© samuel wordley/Alamy)

Exercise-induced asthma is one of the most common conditions among active children, adolescents, and young adults. It occurs in almost 90 percent of people who have chronic asthma and in 40 percent of individuals who have allergic rhinitis or atopic dermatitis.

People who experience exercise-induced asthma should exercise in an environmentally controlled facility and participate in activities that fall within their limitations.

CHAPTER 2

Controversies Concerning Asthma

Vaccines Are a Cause of Asthma

Mark F. Blaxill

Some parents of autistic children have long believed that vaccines caused their children's disorder. With scientific evidence against this belief mounting, advocates continue to spotlight the dangers of vaccination side effects, one of which may be asthma. In the following selection Mark F. Blaxill makes the case for the vaccine-asthma connection. Blaxill, who writes for an online autism parents' advocacy newspaper, focuses on a major Canadian study that finds early vaccination associated with the subsequent development of asthma. The study examined the effect of the triple DPT (diphtheria, pertussis, tetanus) vaccination. Blaxill says the study shows that the earlier a child gets the DPT shot, the higher his or her chances are of developing asthma. Extrapolating from the study's data, Blaxill concludes that a child who gets the vaccination on schedule has a nearly fourfold risk of developing asthma compared with a child who is vaccinated later. He says that the study confirms others conducted by advocacy groups who oppose vaccination and criticizes contrary studies conducted by the federal Centers for Disease Control and Prevention (CDC). Blaxill is a businessman, the father of an autistic child, and editor at large for the *Age of Autism* online newspaper.

Photo on previous page. A scientist in Detroit measures air pollution in an effort to link air quality to the cause of asthma. (© Jim West/Alamy)

SOURCE: Mark F. Blaxill, "Earlier Vaccination Causes Asthma," *Age of Autism*, July 9, 2008. Reproduced by permission.

Lost amidst all the furor over the role of vaccines in autism has been the role that vaccine administration plays in causing other chronic childhood diseases like asthma and juvenile diabetes. But the evidence that vaccine administration, especially early administration of DPT [diphtheria, pertussis, tetanus] vaccine, increases the risk of developing asthma (for the purposes of simplicity, let's shorten that phrase to causes asthma for what follows) is compelling. If you look at the totality of the published evidence the picture is admittedly somewhat mixed, but for anyone with an open mind and a critical eye, the argument for a strong role for vaccines as a cause of asthma is persuasive.

And for any parent trying to figure out whether or not to comply with the aggressive and crowded vaccine schedules, the message from this evidence is simple. Don't comply. Go slower than they want you to. Take responsibility for your own child's health. Because recent research shows not simply that vaccines cause asthma, but that the sooner you give your child some vaccines the higher the odds that your child will develop asthma. These are obviously critical and controversial points, so let's take some time to review some of this research.

A Canadian Study Finds Risks

In a study published earlier this year [2008], a group of Canadian researchers from the University of Manitoba examined the connection between asthma and vaccines in one of the largest studies ever to address the question. What they found was clear and striking. The earlier children received their DPT shots, the higher their odds of developing asthma by their seventh year of age. To be more precise, among children born in Manitoba in 1995 who received their first shot on time (on or before two months of age), nearly 14% subsequently developed asthma. By comparison, among children who received their first shot late (six months or later), less than 6%

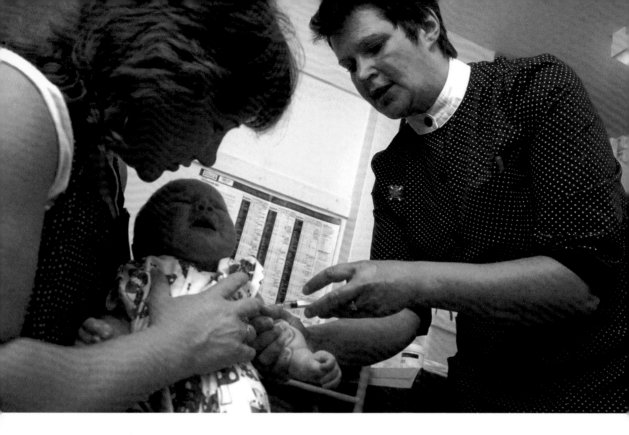

Some studies have shown that children who receive the DPT vaccine on schedule have four times the chance of developing asthma. (© Janine Wiedel Photolibrary/ Alamy)

developed asthma. That's a "crude odds ratio" (before statistical adjustments for "confounders" that might bias the result) of 2.6, meaning that a child vaccinated on schedule is over two and half times more likely to develop asthma than a child vaccinated late. . . .

The basic message is simple. The sooner families in Manitoba lined up to give their children their first DPT shot, the more they raised their child's odds of developing asthma, odds that by my estimate may rise as much as 3–4 times higher once the full range of vaccination timing is considered.

In other words, earlier vaccination causes asthma. . . .

It's also important to recognize that this Canadian study isn't covering virgin territory. Although it's the first to examine the specific question of vaccination timing so carefully (as opposed to a simpler vax/unvax [vaccinated versus unvaccinated children] study design), it's not the first to address the question of vaccination and asthma. Far from it. Indeed there's a long parade of studies, covering many different countries, many different vaccines and using many different study designs. At the highest level, these studies come in two flavors. The first are the less formal vax/unvax surveys, the kind conducted by outsiders to the medical establishment who are worried that the insiders are out of control and not paying attention to the epidemic of chronic disease. Without large resources, prestigious institutions and large research budgets behind them, these efforts pursue the simplest path with the least complexity: they go out and find two populations—one vaccinated and one not—and compare their health outcomes. Time after time, studies like these, whether from our own sponsor Generation Rescue, the Dutch Association for Conscientious Vaccination, or the Immunization Awareness Society in New Zealand, yield similar findings when it comes to asthma. Vaccinated children always have sharply higher risk of developing asthma than unvaccinated children, anywhere from two to six times higher.

There is, of course, another class of study, the kind that makes its way into an indexed medical journal. And although the evidence from this body of work is less consistent than the grass-roots efforts, the weight of evidence among this group of studies is remarkably similar as well. I've read through a large number of them myself and I will summarize them here only briefly. Suffice it to say, there are a number of recognizable patterns in these studies, most of which (like the Manitoba study) focus on the DPT shot. A few (most notably two German studies) actually have shown a protective effect of vaccination. But the majority of them report some kind of elevated asthma risk with vaccination: anywhere from 20% higher to 14 times higher. These studies often draw on smaller samples than the Manitoba study (following hundreds rather than thousands of infants), which is why the Manitoba

FAST FACT

In a University of Manitoba, Canada, study, 13.8 percent of babies who got their first DPT shot at two months of age later developed asthma, compared with 5.9 percent of babies who were four months or older at their first shot.

analysis, with a study population of over 11,000, was so informative.

The CDC Shows a Pro-vaccine Bias

In fact, every study with a sample population larger than 10,000 shows a significant link between vaccines and asthma: every study, that is, except one performed by the CDC [Centers for Disease Control and Prevention] under the guise of the Vaccine Safety Datalink (VSD) program. The CDC has conducted a number of studies on vaccines and asthma. In every case, after deploying elaborate statistical gyrations, . . . the authors conclude

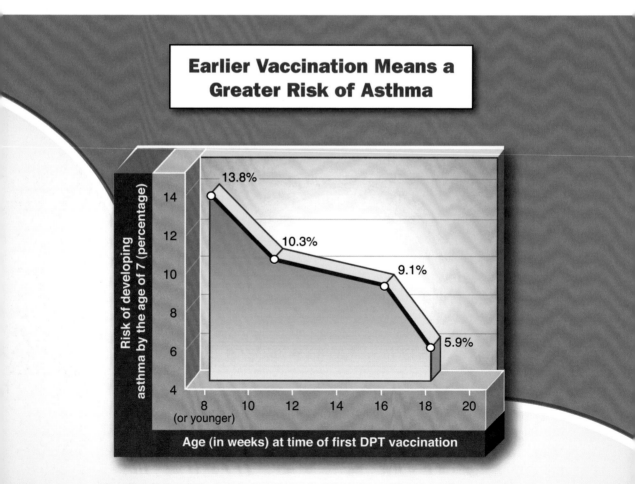

Earlier Vaccination Means a Greater Risk of Asthma

Taken from: Charlotte Bailey, "Delaying Baby Vaccine Could Cut Asthma," *Daily Telegraph*, October 21, 2008. www.telegraph.co.uk/health/3233550/Delaying-baby-vaccine-could-cut-asthma.html.

that vaccines have nothing to do with asthma. The CDC never met a vaccine that made a child sick, so not surprisingly, these studies unfailingly deliver the party line: "do what we tell you to do."

It's important to recognize, however, that the VSD findings go against the weight of evidence. When reading the bulk of the literature, after you cut through the fog of public health propaganda (no one ever says "vaccines cause asthma" in a mainstream medical journal) one cannot help but be persuaded by the weight of evidence. Vaccines cause asthma. So, just like the autism epidemic, the expansion of the vaccine program is likely to have sparked another epidemic of childhood disease. This one, unlike autism, can cause fatal medical complications.

So as evidence mounts for the rising health consequences of the massive human experiment of intensive vaccination launched on this latest generation of children, it has become clear that the debate as it has evolved has become less about the evidence than about belief systems. In a very real way, the proponents of the intensive vaccination experiment want to avoid the usual constraints of health monitoring and safety management because they believe in the project of intensive vaccination as a kind of crusade.

The crusaders in the vaccine development complex view opposition to their programs based on evidence as heresy. Faced with mounting contrary evidence, not only in asthma, but in autism and other neurological conditions, these true believers don't believe in rational dialogue. Instead, as we have seen in recent moves by the AAP [American Academy of Pediatrics], they respond to challenge by intensifying their demands for adherence to their orthodox doctrine. They issue professional fatwas against apostates like Andrew Wakefield [a surgeon who studied the vaccine-autism connection in 1998]. They summon their inner councils to demand that their members take a hard line against rank and file patients who dare to question the sacred programs. And in case there be any inclination for independence of mind within the membership community, the hard liners, zealots like Ayatollah Offit [AAP president Paul Offit], are deployed in an ongoing propaganda blitz to put bright lines of disambiguation out there for any skeptic inclined to stray.

We need to move beyond the religious wars and make it safe again to discuss evidence about vaccine safety, frankly and openly. And a study like the Manitoba effort, if halting in its conclusions is unambiguous in its result. Vaccines cause asthma. It's not a complicated problem, folks, it's what the data are telling us.

The only responsible response to data like this is to act on it. Change the way we administer vaccines. Slow down the schedule. Stop harming children with products and policies that have received insufficient scrutiny. Most of all, we need to recognize that, as a society, promoting the health of today's children and the generations that follow is our highest purpose. At one level, these are rational discussions that rely on data and evidence, but after a time, and at an another level, they become altogether different. And more clear.

The choices we face on children's health are moral choices. Children are being harmed and we must choose to stop it. We must be prepared to face the true believers, rationally and professionally, but with resolve. Our children deserve nothing less.

Vaccines Do Not
Cause Asthma

Stephen Brearey and Rosalind Smyth

The field of pediatrics has dealt with many changes over the past few years. Vaccines have helped to diminish the prevalence of infectious diseases, but childhood health problems, such as asthma, have continued to rise. Stephen Brearey and Rosalind Smyth examine the breakthroughs in recent medicine and explain the use of a new intravenous drug (like a vaccine) for the treatment of asthma. Though some believe vaccines are linked to the cause of asthma, the use of a similar treatment for the disease argues against that belief. Brearey is a clinical researcher at University of Liverpool Institute of Child Health, Alder Hey Children's Hospital, and Smyth is a professor of pediatric medicine in the same institution.

Paediatrics is evolving with the changing health care needs of children in the 21st century. Success of vaccine programmes has led to a decline in admissions for infectious diseases but childhood obesity, diabetes and atopic diseases are more prevalent.

Researchers working on treatments for asthma have found that omalizumab, an intravenous drug (like a vaccine), actually improves asthma symptoms. (© Guy Croft SciTech/Alamy)

Improved survival in childhood malignancies, congenital heart disease, chronic illnesses such as cystic fibrosis and improving neonatal care have all caused increased awareness of long-term morbidity in a larger population of survivors reaching adulthood.

The national service framework [NSF] for children launched [in 2004] hopes to increase the priority given to children in the NHS [National Health Service, the United Kingdom's [UK] national health-care program] and allow the highest standards of care to disseminate throughout the country.

There are key targets to improve child and adolescent mental health services, reduce teenage pregnancy and infant mortality and improve the lives of vulnerable children.

Although the NSF does not have ring-fenced [dedicated] money attached to it, the commitment for change is unprecedented. . . .

Intravenous Drug for Asthma

Recent trials have suggested anti-IgE therapy may be an exciting new treatment for moderate to severe asthma in the future. In the airways of people with asthma, immunoglobulin E (IgE) binds to receptors, predominantly on mast cells and basophils. These events then trigger an inflammatory cascade in the airway. The rationale behind this treatment is that persistent airway inflammation contributes to structural and functional changes in the airways of chronic asthmatics. Early anti-inflammatory therapy may help arrest disease progression as well as improve symptoms.

Anti-IgE antibody (omalizumab), given intravenously or subcutaneously, has been shown to reduce free serum IgE concentrations by more than 90 per cent in adults. Three large double-blind, randomised control trials in adults have shown omalizumab reduces steroid and bronchodilator use and enhances the control of asthma.

A further trial, involving 334 children aged six to 12 years with moderate to severe asthma, compared omalizumab to placebo. In the omalizumab group more participants were able to reduce their steroid dose or to stop inhaled steroids altogether. Participants in the omalizumab group also had fewer exacerbations, hospital admissions and days of missed school.

There have been no reports of serious adverse events related to treatment. Although omalizumab is not yet

> **FAST FACT**
>
> The newer version of the DPT vaccine, known as DPaT (diphtheria, acellular pertussis, and tetanus), has fewer side effects because live cells have been removed from the vaccine, reducing the incidence of adverse reactions to less than 1 percent.

licensed for any age group in the UK, it is now licensed for use in the US for over-12s. Longer-term studies are clearly needed to identify the patients who will benefit most from omalizumab, and to clarify longer-term effects in terms of safety and possible slowing of disease progression. . . .

Anti-IgE antibody therapy for childhood asthma has the exciting potential of improving symptoms and arresting disease progression. Trials in adults have shown it to reduce free serum IgE concentrations by more than 90 per cent and to significantly improve symptoms. More trials in children are needed but it is already licensed in the US for children over 12 years old.

Air Pollution Is a Major Cause of Asthma

Natural Resources Defense Council

Asthma has recently grown to epidemic proportions, and air pollution is a major cause. That is the assertion made in the following selection by the Natural Resources Defense Council (NRDC). According to the advocacy organization, more than half of the U.S. population live in areas where exposure to air pollution is routine. That exposure contributes, the NRDC says, to asthma attacks that keep children out of school and cost the economy billions. Among the pollutants held responsible is particulate matter—tiny particles of soot, ash, and other by-products of combustion. Studies show that such particles are associated with increased hospitalizations of asthma patients, the NRDC says. The organization recommends policy changes to cut down on emissions of pollutants, such as requiring coal-burning power plants to install "air scrubbers" that remove particulates and some other pollutants. It also advocates clean-operating vehicles. The NRDC is a leading environmental action group, combining the grassroots power of 1.2 million members and online activists with the courtroom clout and expertise of more than 350 lawyers, scientists, and other professionals.

SOURCE: Natural Resources Defense Council, "Asthma and Air Pollution," June 8, 2005. www.nrdc.org. Reproduced by permission.

Far too many Americans—about 20 million people—are intimately acquainted with the symptoms of an asthma attack. When asthma strikes, your airways become constricted and swollen, filling with mucus. Your chest feels tight—you may cough or wheeze—and you just can't seem to catch your breath. In severe cases, asthma attacks can be deadly. They kill 5,000 people every year in the United States.

Asthma is a chronic, sometimes debilitating condition that has no cure. It keeps kids out of school (for a total of 14 million lost school days each year, according to the Centers for Disease Control) and sidelines them from physical activity. Employers lose 12 million work days every year when asthma keeps adults out of the workplace. The disease is also responsible for nearly 2 million emergency-room visits a year.

Air pollution monitoring stations have provided data that show a link between air pollution and increased hospitalizations of asthma patients.
(© Jim West/Alamy)

Understanding what might trigger an asthma attack helps asthma sufferers keep their disease in check. Sometimes it's as simple as avoiding dust, tobacco smoke or cockroach droppings. But what if the air outside your home is filled with asthma triggers?

In recent years, scientists have shown that air pollution from cars, factories and power plants is a major cause of asthma attacks. And more than 159 million Americans—over half the nation's population—live in areas with bad air. A research study published in 2002 estimated that 30 percent of childhood asthma is due to environmental exposures, costing the nation $2 billion per year. And studies also suggest that air pollution may contribute to the development of asthma in previously healthy people.

Air Pollutants That Trigger Asthma

• Ground Level Ozone: A toxic component of smog, ozone triggers asthma attacks and makes existing asthma worse. It may also lead to the development of asthma in children. Ozone is produced at ground level when tailpipe pollution from cars and trucks reacts with oxygen and sunlight. Ground level ozone is a big problem in cities with lots of traffic, such as Los Angeles, Houston and New York City. In 2004, according to the American Lung Association, 136 million people lived in areas that violated ozone air quality standards.

• Sulfur Dioxide (SO_2): A respiratory irritant associated with the onset of asthma attacks, sulfur dioxide is produced when coal and crude oil are burned. Coal-fired power plants, particularly older plants that burn coal without SO_2 pollution controls, are the worst SO_2 polluters. One in five Americans lives within 10 miles of a coal-fired power plant. Oil refineries and diesel engines that burn high-sulfur fuel also release large amounts of SO_2 into the air.

• Particulate Matter: This term refers to a wide range of pollutants—dust, soot, fly ash, diesel exhaust particles, wood smoke and sulfate aerosols—which are suspended as tiny particles in the air. Some of these fine particles can become lodged in the lungs and could trigger asthma attacks. Studies have shown that the number of hospitalizations for asthma increases when levels of particulate matter in the air rise. Coal-fired power plants, factories and diesel vehicles are major sources of particulate pollution. Around 81 million people live in areas that fail to meet national air quality standards for particulate matter.

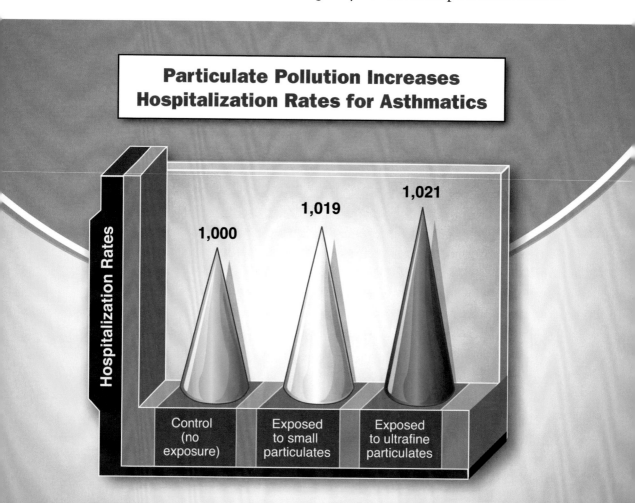

Taken from: F.W.O. Ko, "Effects of Air Pollution on Asthma Hospitalization Rates in Different Age Groups in Hong Kong," *Clinical & Experimental Allergy*, September 2007. http://lib.bioinfo.pl/pmid:17845411.

• Nitrogen oxide (NO_x): A gas emitted from tailpipes and power plants, nitrogen oxide contributes to the formation of ground-level ozone and smog. It also reacts with other air pollutants to form small particles that can cause breathing difficulties, especially in people with asthma.

The Air Quality Index

If you have asthma, your doctor can help you design a plan to control and prevent asthma attacks. Limiting your exposure to air pollution can be an important part of that plan. The EPA [Environmental Protection Agency] keeps tabs on local air quality across the country through its daily Air Quality Index, which measures levels of five major air pollutants.

Check the EPA website or your local television, newspaper or radio weather reports for daily updates on air quality. On bad air days, signified by orange and red colors on the index, children and people with respiratory diseases should limit their time outdoors. Purple and maroon indicate extreme levels of pollution—even healthy adults should try to stay inside.

> **FAST FACT**
>
> The hospitalization of asthmatic children jumped by 31 percent from 1994 to 2004.

Although air quality has improved in many areas of the country over the past 15 years, air pollution still poses a health risk for millions of Americans. Adopting stricter national air quality standards for particulate matter and ozone would help clear the air by giving states a stronger tool to force polluters to clean up; it would also encourage industry to switch to cleaner fuels as an alternative to dirty diesel—diesel exhaust has been linked to asthma as well as cancer. Requiring coal-fired power plants that operate without SO_2 controls to install scrubbers to curb their emissions would also help reduce health risks for asthma sufferers and people who live near these polluting facilities. And putting more clean-running, fuel-efficient cars and trucks on the road can cut down on emissions of NO_x and other chemicals that contribute to ozone formation.

Air Pollution Is Not a Major Cause of Wintertime Asthma

William Allstetter

There are many suspected causes of asthma, but according to the following selection, one suspect can be crossed off the list. William Allstetter states that a study published in the *Journal of Allergy and Clinical Immunology* shows that tiny particles suspended in the air do not contribute in a significant way to asthma among elementary school children. The study looked at more than one hundred children enrolled in Denver schools during the winter, when so-called particulate air pollution reaches its maximum. The pollution did have adverse effects on the health of the children, but a careful statistical analysis to isolate pollution's effect on asthma found no significant causal connection. Other kinds of pollution, from the gases carbon monoxide and ozone, made only a tiny increase in the odds of a child having an asthma attack. However, the study leaves open the possibility that summertime pollution may act differently on childhood asthma. Allstetter is the director of media and external relations at the National Jewish Medical & Research Center in Denver, Colorado.

SOURCE: William Allstetter, "Respiratory Infections, Not Air Pollution, Pose Winter Health Threat for Children with Asthma," National Jewish Medical & Research Center, November 9, 2004. Reproduced by permission.

Although particulate air pollution has been blamed for a wide variety of negative health effects, a three-year study of asthmatic children in Denver, published in the November [2004] *Journal of Allergy and Clinical Immunology*, indicates that it does not lead to significant worsening of asthma during the pollution-heavy winter months. Upper respiratory infections, however, were associated with a significant decline in lung function, asthma symptoms and asthma exacerbations.

"In our study, wintertime air pollution had no significant effect on asthma exacerbations or lung function," said Nathan Rabinovitch, M.D., a lead author of the study and pediatric allergist at National Jewish

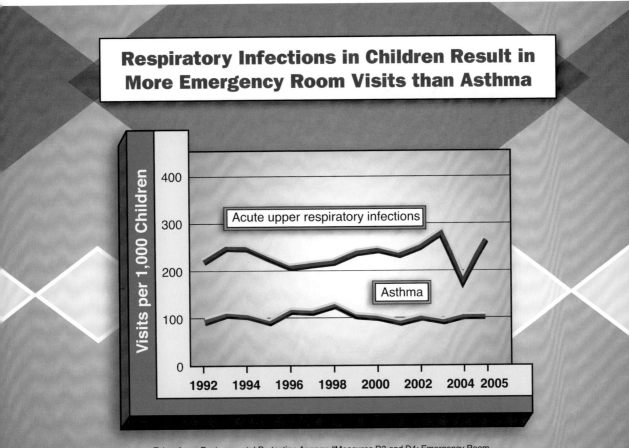

Respiratory Infections in Children Result in More Emergency Room Visits than Asthma

Taken from: Environmental Protection Agency, "Measures D3 and D4: Emergency Room Visits and Hospitalizations for Respiratory Diseases," November 1, 2007.

Medical and Research Center. "Upper respiratory infections, however, doubled the chances that a child would suffer an asthma exacerbation and more than quadrupled the odds that a child would suffer asthma symptoms."

Elementary School Kids Monitored

The study monitored 41, 63 and 43 elementary school children during three successive winters in Denver, Colorado, when particulate pollution is worst. The children, aged 6 to 12 years, were mostly urban minority children with moderate to severe asthma. Dr. Rabinovitch and co-investigator Erwin Gelfand, M.D., Chairman of Pediatrics at National Jewish, monitored several health outcomes in the children, including asthma exacerbations, visits to emergency rooms and hospitalizations. They also monitored the children's lung function, medication use, asthma symptoms, and whether they had upper respiratory infections.

The researchers correlated those health measures with daily variations in six air pollutants: particulates less than 10 microns in diameter, particulates less than 2.5 microns in diameter, carbon monoxide, nitrogen dioxide, sulfur dioxide and ozone. In general, pollutants were comparable to levels found in most large American cities.

As expected, the raw data did show worse health associated with high pollution days. But when the researchers controlled for potential time-related confounders, such as upper respiratory infections, the correlation disappeared on almost all measures. Higher carbon monoxide levels were marginally associated with increased use of rescue medications (odds ratio: 1.065) and daily symptoms were marginally associated with ozone levels (odds ratio: 1.083).

"It is well known that upper respiratory infections can cause problems for people with asthma, but the air pollutions results were a surprise," said Dr. Gelfand. "We be-

> **FAST FACT**
>
> A 2006 study of asthmatic schoolchildren under similar conditions in Fresno, California, also found no causal connection between air pollution and asthma.

lieve that careful monitoring of the children allowed us to filter out confounding factors that would have mistakenly suggested a significant health impact of air pollution."

A chemist looks at a sample, left, of particulate matter collected from the air. The sample is used to determine the amount of particle pollution in the air. (**AP Images**)

The Summer May Tell a Different Story

The researchers are not ready to write off the effects of air pollution during summer. For one, children may be exposed to higher levels of air pollution in the summer because they spend more time outside. Also, ozone, a known respiratory irritant, rises to much higher levels during the summer and may pose more of a problem than particulate pollution in the winter. Next summer [2005] Drs. Rabinovitch and Gelfand will begin a study of the health impacts of ozone on children with asthma.

"We believe this is good news for parents of children with asthma," said Rabinovitch. "Instead of worrying about air pollution they can focus their efforts on preventing and treating the real wintertime threat to their children's health—colds and other respiratory infections."

Food Allergies Are a Major Factor in Asthma

Gale Jurasek

In the following selection Gale Jurasek examines the connections between food allergies and asthma. Citing a British study, Jurasek says the evidence suggests that food allergies can contribute to a life-threatening exacerbation of asthma. The study, which followed nineteen children who were admitted to a hospital for asthma treatment, found that food allergies boosted the risk of a severe relapse by nearly sixfold. Children with food allergies also failed to respond to treatment as well as the asthmatic children who did not have food allergies. Scientists admit they still have not traced the pathways connecting food allergies and asthma. It is possible, says one, that airborne food particles are responsible for the extra risk. In any event, they say that food allergy is clearly a factor that requires special attention in an asthmatic child. Jurasek is a medical writer with *Respiratory Reviews*. She was previously an editor at *Exceptional Parent* magazine.

SOURCE: Gale Jurasek, "Do Food Allergies Interact with Life-Threatening Asthma?" *Respiratory Reviews,* October 2003. Reproduced by permission of Quadrant HealthCom Inc.

Allergies can exacerbate asthma and make symptom control more difficult. Although food allergies can produce respiratory symptoms, their role in life-threatening asthma has not been examined in detail, nor has the relationship between the lungs and gut in the context of food allergy and asthma been well studied. Recently, however, researchers in the United Kingdom found that in children, a combination of poor asthma control and food allergy can greatly increase the risk of a life-threatening asthma exacerbation.

They conducted a case-control study of 19 children (ages 1 to 16) who were admitted to a pediatric ICU [intensive care unit] with severe asthma that required ventilation and 38 children—two for each case patient—who were admitted to the emergency department (ED) with asthma. All of the children were asked about exposure to food allergens and symptoms of anaphylaxis [allergic shock] within the 24 hours prior to their asthma exacerbation.

Children were assessed between 18 and 20 months after their initial hospitalization or ED admission. At this time, forced expiratory volume in one second (FEV1) and forced vital capacity (FVC) were measured before and 15 minutes after administration of twice the usual dose of a bronchodilator. Skin testing was performed for grass and tree pollens, molds, dog, cat, and house dust mite. In addition, specific immunoglobulin E to common food allergies was measured.

Food Allergy Was a Major Factor

Food allergy, which was present in 10 cases and four controls, was a significant risk factor for life-threatening asthma; it increased the risk of a severe exacerbation almost sixfold. The average number of diagnoses for other allergies was 3.58 and 2.73 among cases and controls, respectively. The presence of more than three allergies increased the risk of life-threatening asthma. . . .

Doctors treating children for asthma have found a connection between food allergies and the risk of developing asthma. (© Phototake Inc./Alamy)

Among the cases, FEV1 (as a percentage of predicted) was 81% after treatment with oral and inhaled corticosteroids, compared with 93.4% among the control group. There was a trend toward reduced bronchodilator reversibility in the case group as well.

"It is difficult to know what caused the decline in lung function and reduced bronchodilator response," said Gideon Lack, Senior Lecturer and Consultant in Pediatric Allergy and Immunology at St. Mary's Hospital in London. "Decreased lung function with a poor bronchodilator response in asthma despite adequate anti-inflammatory treatment is suggestive of airway remodeling.". . .

According to the authors, more than one third of children with food allergies have asthma, and as many as 8% of children with asthma have food allergies.

What are some possible explanations for the apparent relationship between food allergy and life-threatening asthma? "There isn't really a clear-cut connection between the gut and the respiratory tract as there appears to be between the upper and lower respiratory tract," admitted John M. James, MD, an allergy and immunology specialist at the Colorado Allergy and Asthma Centers in Fort Collins. "There are allergic reactions that can be isolated to the lung or gut, and there are also systemic anaphylactic reactions, which can involve the skin, intestines, and

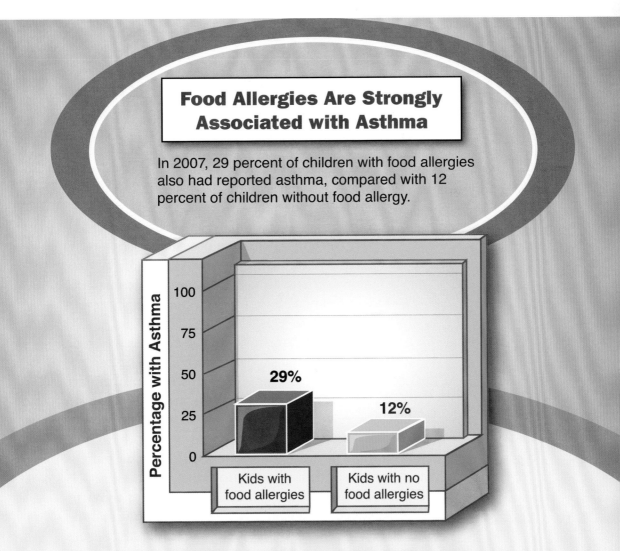

Food Allergies Are Strongly Associated with Asthma

In 2007, 29 percent of children with food allergies also had reported asthma, compared with 12 percent of children without food allergy.

Taken from: *U.S. News & World Report*, "Food Allergies Up 18% Among U.S. Children," October 22, 2007. http://health.usnews.com/articles/health/healthday/2008/10/22/food-allergies-up-18-among-us-children.html.

lungs." The type of reaction a patient will have is highly variable and, Dr. James pointed out, "It isn't easy to predict what will happen—particularly if the patient has not had a similar reaction in the past."

Airborne Food Allergens

"The important point is that food allergy has been artificially separated from inhalant allergies," said Dr. Lack. "Thus, food allergies are seen to cause gastrointestinal symptoms, and inhalant allergies, respiratory symptoms." Instead, Dr. Lack suggested that physicians be aware that "food allergens can behave like inhalant allergens in the sense that they can become aerosolized in the environment and cause only late-phase responses." An example of this would be vapors from boiling seafood.

> **FAST FACT**
>
> More than three times as many children than adults suffer from both food allergies and asthma. One reason is that about half of all asthmatic children outgrow their condition.

Whatever the mechanism, control of asthma symptoms is critical in patients with coexistent asthma and food allergy. "If someone has poorly managed asthma, there may be a diminished bronchodilator response over time," said Dr. James. This can be seen in people with occupational asthma, he observed. If they remain in their current jobs and are constantly exposed to asthma triggers, their lung function will decline.

Dr. Lack suggested that food allergy may be an indicator or biological marker for children who are susceptible to severe asthma. "Perhaps the most important message is that special attention should be given to children who have food allergies and asthma."

"Today," said Dr. James, "one question that clinicians should ask if they have a chronic asthma patient who is not responding to appropriate treatment is, 'Is there a food allergy exposure?' Features that may indicate the need for evaluation of food allergy include recalcitrant or otherwise unexplained acute, severe asthma, asthma triggered after ingestion of a specific food, and asthma that is accompanied by other manifestations of food allergy (eg, moderate to severe atopic dermatitis or anaphylaxis)."

It is important to keep in mind that patients can have severe anaphylaxis without asthma, and vice versa. However, Dr. James added, "patients with asthma are a higher-risk group for anaphylaxis than those without asthma."

Food Allergies Are Not a Major Factor in Asthma

International Food Information Council Foundation

Allergies are strongly associated with asthma. However, a controversy exists about whether food allergies in particular are a cause of asthma. In the following selection the International Food Information Council Foundation asserts that the causal connection is weak and that food allergies have been confused with food sensitivities, as well as with food additives. The foundation first describes food allergies and explains how the body reacts to "true" food allergens—as opposed to certain additives and preservatives which, though they may trigger asthma, are not to be considered food allergens. Aside from these additives, the foundation says, only a few actual foods have been scientifically demonstrated to trigger asthma. Nevertheless, the foundation advises people with asthma and food allergies to play it safe; they should avoid the ingredients to which they may be allergic. The foundation is the educational arm of the International Food Information Council (IFIC), whose mission is to communicate science-based information on food safety and nutrition to health and nutrition professionals, educators, journalists, government officials, and others providing information to consumers. IFIC is supported primarily by the food, beverage, and agricultural industries.

SOURCE: International Food Information Council Foundation, "Backgrounder: Food Allergies & Asthma," November 2006. ific.org. Reprinted with permission from the International Food Information Council Foundation, 2009.

A food allergy is an adverse reaction to a food or food component that involves the body's immune system. A true allergic reaction to a food involves three primary components: 1) contact with a food allergen (reaction-provoking substance, virtually always a protein); 2) immunoglobulin E (IgE—an antibody in the immune system that reacts with allergens); and 3) mast cells (tissue cells) and basophils (blood cells), which when connected to IgE antibodies release histamine or other substances causing allergic symptoms.

The body's immune system recognizes an allergen in a food as foreign and produces antibodies to halt the "invasion." As the battle rages, symptoms appear throughout the body. The most common reaction sites are the mouth (swelling of the lips), digestive tract (stomach cramps, vomiting, diarrhea), skin (hives, rashes, or eczema), and the airways (wheezing or breathing problems).

Fish is one of the "Big 8" group of food allergens. The group also includes shellfish, milk, eggs, soy, wheat, peanuts, and tree nuts. (© Richard Levine/Alamy)

Allergic reactions to food are rare and can be caused by any food. The most common food allergens, known as the "Big 8," are fish, shellfish, milk, egg, soy, wheat, peanuts, and tree nuts such as walnuts, cashews, etc. Symptoms of a food allergy are highly individual and usually begin within minutes to a few hours after eating the offending food. People with true, confirmed food allergies must avoid the offending food altogether.

Food Allergies Versus Other Allergies and Intolerance

There are numerous misconceptions regarding allergy to food additives, preservatives, and ingredients. Although some additives and preservatives have been shown to trigger asthma or hives in certain people, these reactions are not the same as those reactions observed with food allergies. These reactions do not involve the immune system and therefore are examples of food intolerance or idiosyncrasy rather than food allergy. Most people consume a wide variety of food additives and ingredients daily, with only a very small number having been associated with adverse reactions.

There are also some adverse reactions to foods that involve the body's metabolism but not the immune system. These reactions are known as food intolerance. Examples of food intolerance are food poisoning or the inability to properly digest certain food components, such as lactose or milk sugar. This latter condition is commonly known as lactose intolerance. . . .

If a food allergy is diagnosed, the only proven therapy is avoidance of the offending food. Because there are no drugs or allergy shots on the market today to alter the long-term course of food allergy, elimination diets are prescribed. Each diet must consider the person's individual nutritional needs—ability to tol-

> **FAST FACT**
>
> One food additive known to trigger asthma in some people is sulfite. Commonly added to wines, cooked fruits and shellfish, and some medications, as little as one part of sulfite per million can bring on an asthma attack in some people.

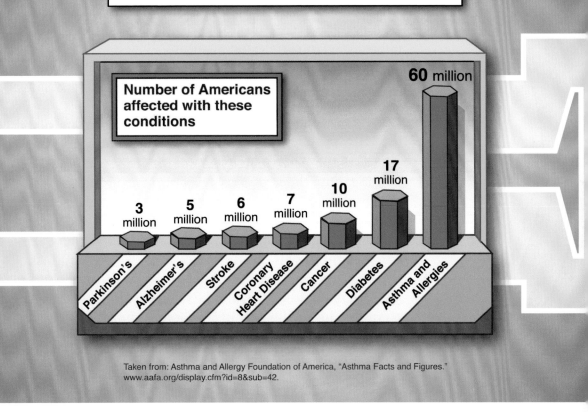

Asthma and Allergies Together Form the Most Common Chronic Malady

Number of Americans affected with these conditions

Parkinson's	Alzheimer's	Stroke	Coronary Heart Disease	Cancer	Diabetes	Asthma and Allergies
3 million	5 million	6 million	7 million	10 million	17 million	60 million

Taken from: Asthma and Allergy Foundation of America, "Asthma Facts and Figures." www.aafa.org/display.cfm?id=8&sub=42.

erate the offending food, caloric needs, and other factors. Strict adherence to an elimination diet and careful avoidance of the food allergen may, in some cases, hasten the disappearance of the food allergy.

Asthma and Food

Asthma, a chronic medical condition, affects more than 17 million Americans (three to four percent of the population). Asthma results when triggers (or irritants) cause swelling of the tissues to the air passages of the lungs, making it difficult to breathe. Typical symptoms of asthma include wheezing, coughing, and shortness of breath.

Asthma can be triggered by numerous factors, including allergens from dust, molds, pollen, animals, and, occasionally, food; air pollutants, such as cigarette smoke, auto exhaust, smog, or aerosol cleaners; colds and, particularly, respiratory infections; weather changes; exercise; or certain medications.

Food-triggered asthma is rare, occurring only among six to eight percent of children with asthma and less than two percent of adults with asthma. . . .

For years it has been suspected that foods or food ingredients may cause or exacerbate symptoms in those with asthma. After many years of scientific and clinical investigation, there are very few confirmed food triggers of asthma. Sulfites and sulfiting agents in foods (found in dried fruits, prepared potatoes, wine, bottled lemon or lime juice, and shrimp), and diagnosed food allergens (such as milk, eggs, peanuts, tree nuts, soy, wheat, fish, and shellfish) have been found to trigger asthma. Many food ingredients such as food dyes and colors, food preservatives like BHA and BHT, monosodium glutamate, aspartame, and nitrite, have not been conclusively linked to asthma.

The best way to avoid food-induced asthma is to eliminate or avoid the offending food or food ingredient from the diet or from the environment. Reading ingredient information on food labels and knowing where food triggers of asthma are found are the best defenses against a food-induced asthma attack. The main objectives of an asthmatic's care and treatment are to stay healthy, to remain symptom free, to enjoy food, to exercise, to use medications properly, and to follow the care plan developed between the physician and patient.

Controversy Lingers over Asthma Drug Safety

Steven Reinberg

The use of drugs to treat asthma is essential, but drugs carry risks. In the following selection Steven Reinberg reports on a controversial decision by a U.S. Food and Drug Administration (FDA) panel about the risks and benefits of four asthma drugs. The panel ruled that two of the drugs have benefits that outweigh the risks, and two are more risky than helpful. Two widely used anti-asthma drugs, Advair and Symbicort, got through without restrictions. However, a majority of the expert panel voted to put restrictions on two other drugs, Serevent and Foradil. One area that the panel had no trouble agreeing about was the question of whether the drugs were safe enough for children. The panelists voted unanimously that they are not. The votes left other experts divided. Some point to thousands of deaths that may have resulted from use—or misuse—of the flagged drugs as reason to ban them. Others say that even more deaths from asthma would have occurred had the drugs not been available. Reinberg reports on health and medicine for *HealthDay*.

SOURCE: Steven Reinberg, "Two Asthma Meds May Be Too Risky, FDA Panel Says," *Washington Post*, December 11, 2008. Copyright © 2008 Scout News LLC. All rights reserved. Reproduced by permission of the author.

The risks of two widely used asthma drugs outweigh their benefits for both children and adults, a U.S. Food and Drug Administration [FDA] advisory panel said [December 11, 2008].

The health panel targeted [drug company] Glaxo-SmithKline's Serevent and Foradil, made jointly by Novartis AG and Schering-Plough, for restrictions, but it excluded Advair, Glaxo's biggest-selling drug in the class of medications known as long-acting beta-agonists. It also left alone a fourth such drug, AstraZeneca's Symbicort.

The health experts did not say that the use of Serevent and Foradil should be abandoned altogether. Instead, they said the medications' labeling should be reworded to urge doctors to use the drugs along with an inhaled corticosteroid—as guidelines already recommend.

That may help explain why Advair and Symbicort were spared. Serevent contains just one active ingredient, salmeterol, while Foradil contains only formoterol. Advair is a combination of both salmeterol and fluticasone (an inhaled cortocosteroid), while Symbicort contains formoterol and another steroid (budesonide). All of these drugs relax airway muscles, letting asthma patients breathe more easily.

Controversy over Deaths

The controversy over these drugs has been going on for several years, with two FDA officials recently calling for banning the use of these drugs for anyone under 17. The results of studies noting a rise in asthma-related deaths by people using the medications have already resulted in a black-box warning that use could "increase the risk of asthma-related death."

The advisory panel voted 10 to 17 on whether the benefits of Serevent outweighed its risk as maintenance therapy for adults, and voted 6 to 21 on the same question for adolescents ages 12 to 17, [news service] Dow

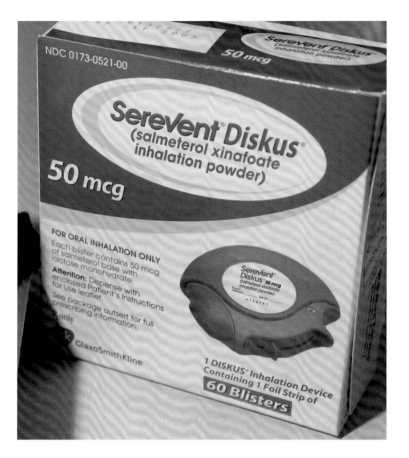

In 2008 the federal Food and Drug Administration strongly recommended that the widely used asthma drug Serevent not be given to children aged eleven or younger.
(Tannen Maury/Bloomberg News/Landov)

Jones reported. Foradil received similar votes on the same questions: 9 to 18 for adults and 6 to 21 for adults.

The panelists were unanimous in voting that the benefits of the two drugs did not outweigh risks when used for children ages 11 and younger.

The announcement followed a two-day meeting on the issue by the expert advisory panel. The FDA is not obligated to follow the advice of its advisory panels but usually does so.

Speaking before [the] decision, one expert said the problem is not with the drugs, but with their misuse.

"This is an over-interpretation of the risk without adequate consideration of benefit," said Dr. Miles Weinberger, a professor of pediatrics at the University of Iowa.

"However, there has been irresponsible marketing of the products, salmeterol and formoterol, and irresponsible prescribing by many physicians."

"Since most patients with chronic asthma can be controlled with inhaled steroids alone, using these more expensive combination formulations as first line is inap-

Study Finds an Increase in Deaths Associated with the Drug Serevent

During a 28-week study, 13 people died out of 13,176 asthma patients on the drug Serevent, which contains salmeterol, and only 3 people died out of 13,179 asthma patients on a placebo.

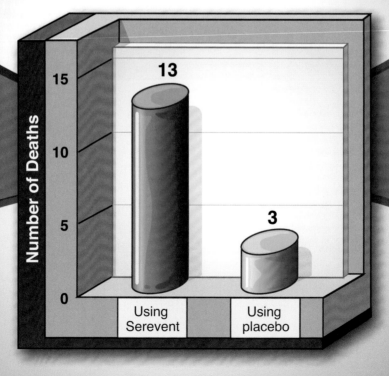

Taken from: FDA, "Serevent Diskus: Warning," May 25, 2006. www.fda.gov/cder/foi/label/2006/020692s029lbl.pdf.

propriate but strongly encouraged by marketing practices" of drug makers, Weinberger said.

In the panel's first day of hearings on [December 10, 2008], FDA officials themselves were split over the risks of the drugs.

Deaths Result Either Way

One official told the panel members that more than 14,000 people may have died since 1994 after taking the drugs, while another suggested that an even greater number might have died without them, according to *The New York Times.*

[Prior to the hearings in December 2008], two FDA officials, who work in the agency's safety division, posted an assessment on the agency Web site, saying asthma sufferers of all ages should not take the medicines. But a third FDA official concluded that Advair and Symbicort are safe for adults, but that all four drugs should no longer be used by children 17 and younger, the *Times* said.

The panel was reviewing an FDA study of 110 trials that included 60,954 people and found an increase in asthma-related hospitalization, asthma-related intubation, and asthma-related death in asthmatic patients with the use of these drugs. The risk varied, however, depending on the particular drug studied.

For example, there were 20 asthma-related deaths, 16 among people taking long-acting beta agonists compared with four patients not taking these drugs. All the deaths were in patients taking Serevent, the FDA notes.

The increased risk wasn't seen when a long-acting beta agonist was used along with an inhaled corticosteroid, the agency found.

> **FAST FACT**
>
> Four major classes of drugs are used to treat asthma: bronchodilators, which open airways; anti-inflammatory drugs, which reduce inflammation; leukotriene blockers, which reduce the body's production of a substance that contributes to inflammation; and anti-IgE medications, which dampen allergic reactions.

The Risk Is Highest for Children

The greatest risk appears to be among children aged 4 to 11; women also appeared to be at greater risk than men.

Weinberger thinks that long-acting beta agonists should be used only in combination with inhaled steroids. "All trials of the combination of long-acting beta agonists and an inhaled steroid demonstrate substantial additive effect for patients not fully controlled on the inhaled steroid alone," Weinberger said. "The sensible approach is to use the combination products only after inadequate control is observed with an inhaled steroid alone."

For their part, the drugs' manufacturers said they believe there is adequate evidence that their products are safe and effective when used properly. In a joint statement issued after the panel voted, Novartis and Schering-Plough said both companies "remain confident in the safety and efficacy of Foradil." The statement added, "Novartis and Schering-Plough strongly disagree with the Joint Advisory Committee's view that the benefits of Foradil do not outweigh its risks in patients using it according to current product labeling for the maintenance treatment of asthma. We believe this opinion is inconsistent with clinical evidence supporting the benefit/risk profile of Foradil in patients not adequately controlled on other asthma-controller treatments."

CHAPTER 3

Personal Experiences with Asthma

Personal Accounts of Asthma

Kathiann M. Kowalski

In the following viewpoint Kathiann M. Kowalski describes (now retired) Pittsburgh Steelers running back Jerome Bettis's experiences with asthma, along with those of others who suffer with the disease Though each patient has asthma, Kowalski takes care to point out that the triggers of an asthma attack vary with the individual. For example, Christopher Safrath suffers most when dust and pine are present, while Bethany Meissner's attacks are triggered by smoke. The article points out that, although asthma is on the rise and many suffer from the disease, with the right kind of action plan and support system, it can be controlled. Kowalski is a writer and contributor to *Current Health 2.*

Few things could stop Pittsburgh Steelers running back Jerome "The Bus" Bettis. Then a severe asthma attack struck during a nationally televised game against the Jacksonville Jaguars.

Photo on previous page. Asthma sufferers must learn to live as normally as possible with their affliction. (© DonSmith/Landov)

SOURCE: Kathiann M. Kowalski, "Asthma Alert: Asthma Is a Life-Threatening Disease. When a Member of the Family Has It, All Family Members Are Affected," *Current Health 2,* a Weekly Reader publication, November 2002. Reproduced by permission.

Professional football player Jerome Bettis, formerly a running back for the Pittsburgh Steelers, was diagnosed with asthma at age fifteen. **(Michael Tullberg/Getty Images)**

"I was on the field, and I just couldn't breathe," Jerome recalled. As both his parents watched from the stands, medics carried Jerome off the field. With doctors' help and his family's support, Jerome got his asthma back under control with a daily action plan.

Jerome was fortunate. The Centers for Disease Control and Prevention (CDC) says asthma causes about 5,000 deaths annually. Plus, asthma is affecting record numbers of teens and their families.

Defining Asthma and Its Triggers

Asthma is a chronic, or long-term, disease that interferes with the ability to breathe. Medicine can treat the disease, but it doesn't go away. Asthma is always there, even when patients feel good.

Asthma patients' lungs are super-sensitive, or "twitchy." Inflammation swells the lining of the lungs' airways and shrinks air passages. During an asthma attack or episode, muscles surrounding the airways tighten, causing bronchospasm. Mucus and fluid clog airways too.

People experience asthma episodes in different ways. Wheezing was Jerome Bettis's first symptom. Doctors first diagnosed his asthma around age 15.

Eighteen-year-old Bethany Meissner coughs nonstop when her asthma acts up. "I have to stop whatever I'm doing because I can't breathe properly," she says. "It's very frustrating." Sometimes Bethany's parents hear her hacking at 2 a.m. Mucus and fluid tend to accumulate in lungs overnight.

FAST FACT

Weather may cause problems for people with asthma in any climate. Weather that may worsen asthma symptoms includes extremely hot or cold temperatures, windy conditions, changes in the humidity, or shifts in barometric pressure.

For 16-year-old Shannon Walker, "It seems like someone is closing your chest and you can't breathe or anything." Other people feel like they just can't catch their breath. They may feel out of shape or exhausted much of the time.

Just as symptoms vary, so do asthma triggers. For 16-year-old Christopher Safrath, "Dust, pine, and usually cats are big offenders."

Indoor molds set off Bethany's asthma. Her asthma also gets worse when she has a cold or flu. Cigarette smoke probably irritates Bethany the most.

"I can't stay around my grandma when she smokes," Bethany says. "I don't want to hurt anyone's feelings, but I have to breathe." Of course, smoking is bad for everyone—whether a person has asthma or not!

Pollen bothers many people with asthma during spring and summer. Outdoor molds make things worse for other patients during summer and fall. Air pollutants like ground-level ozone, sulfur dioxide, and particulates can also irritate asthma patients' lungs. Even cold air can trigger asthma attacks.

Besides molds and dust mites, possible indoor triggers include cockroaches, cleansers, dogs, perfume, and certain foods. Even exercise—as good as it is for everyone—triggers asthma attacks for some patients.

An Increase in Asthma Cases

Allergy & Asthma Network Mothers of Asthmatics says more than 17 million Americans have asthma. That's more than twice the 1980 estimate of around 7 million Americans. Studies suggest different theories for the increase.

Better-insulated homes, for example, trap more molds and dust inside. A couch-potato lifestyle can mean more time spent indoors—and thus more exposure to potential triggers. Another theory is that overuse of antibiotics has impaired some patients' immune systems.

Poverty plays a role too. Low-income housing in many cities is deteriorating. That may mean more cockroaches and other pests to trigger asthma.

Diagnostic methods have improved too. In any event, the CDC says asthma is a "key public health problem." Because asthma can be fatal, patients must get it under control.

Dealing with Asthma

The first step in dealing with asthma is getting the disease diagnosed. The second step is identifying a patient's particular triggers. Sometimes doctors can figure out when asthma attacks typically occur. Other times, doctors need more detailed testing, such as skin patch tests for possible allergens.

Once they've identified triggers, doctors help patients develop a strategy to keep asthma under control. When the strategy is working, dealing with asthma should be almost as easy as ABC.

"A" is for Avoidance. Common sense says that if something bothers your health, you avoid it. Thus, some families must give away pets. Others eliminate carpets, feather pillows, or other items likely to harbor dust mites or other triggers.

Unfortunately, avoidance isn't always possible. Then, asthma patients rely on Plan "B": Be prepared. Asthma patients often carry inhalers with them in case of an attack. Rescue medicines inside inhalers relax muscles and dilate airways. This helps the patient's breathing return to normal. (People react to medicines differently, so never share inhalers.)

Being prepared is good; preventing emergencies is better. Thus, "C" is for controller medicines. Asthma patients don't feel any immediate change from these medicines. In fact, they may take days or weeks to work. Taken every day, however, these "quiet medicines" reduce inflammation in the lungs. Thus, they control the underlying process, rather than just acute symptoms. Some controller medicines also counter the body's response to different allergens.

Asthma is a serious, possibly life-threatening disease. And, while symptoms and sensitivity can change over time, the disease doesn't go away.

If you have asthma, learn about the disease, and follow the control strategy that your doctor recommends. That way, you'll be able to tackle asthma head-on.

Family Support

Asthma and allergies affect Shannon Walker's whole family. Both her older brother and sister have asthma and allergies too. Her parents have made major lifestyle changes to improve their children's health.

When Shannon was little, the family lived on a farm in Michigan. Then they learned that chicken, goose, and

The Ten Worst Places in the United States for Asthma Sufferers to Live

Rank	Asthma Risk Score	City
1	100.00	Knoxville, TN
2	95.49	Tulsa, OK
3	91.21	Milwaukee, WI
4	90.63	Atlanta, GA
5	90.07	Memphis, TN
6	89.89	Allentown, PA
7	88.34	Charlotte, NC
8	87.84	Greenville, SC
9	87.53	Saint Louis, MO
10	86.79	Greensboro, NC

Taken from: Asthma and Allergy Foundation of America, "2008 Asthma Capitals—the Most Challenging Places to Live with Asthma," 2008. http://aafa.org/pdfs/FinalPublicList_AC_2008.pdf.

turkey feathers triggered the oldest child's asthma. Except for the dog, the family got rid of all the animals. They sold the farm and moved into a house with wood floors.

Avoiding triggers seems hard at first. But, says Shannon, "As you get used to it, it just becomes part of your lifestyle." When springtime pollen, high ozone, or fall molds make Shannon's asthma worse, for example, she steps up her asthma plan so she can continue normal routines.

Despite having asthma, Shannon stays active. She runs a lot. She also enjoys swimming, in-line skating, tennis, and other sports. "Being active is important because it makes your lungs stronger," stresses Shannon.

Shannon's parents do everything they can to help. Yet they encourage all their children to "take ownership" of their asthma. "Wherever they go, they need to take all they've learned over the last 10 or 12 years and make sure they can breathe," stresses their mom. "Breathing is pretty basic, and they're in charge of it!"

"Don't let asthma get to you," adds Shannon. "Be aware of it, but don't let it slow you down."

Healthier than an Olympic Swimmer

Nancy Hogshead

In the following selection Nancy Hogshead, winner of three gold medals at the 1984 Olympics, reveals that she was one of hundreds of Olympians who have asthma. During the ten years she was training for the Olympics, she frequently got sick and battled a cough, but in all that time she never imagined that it was asthma. When a doctor finally diagnosed her, she reacted with incredulity. For a time she tried going without an inhaler and other asthma management techniques, but the condition laid her low. After being hospitalized as a result of her asthma, she became serious about taking her medicines and avoiding triggers. Eventually, she learned to manage her disease so well that she was able to resume outdoor sports without difficulty. Today, she says, she is actually healthier than when she was competing in the Olympics. Hogshead won four swimming medals in all at the 1984 Olympics—three gold and one silver. She went on to become a successful attorney and then joined the law faculty of the Florida Coastal School of Law.

SOURCE: Nancy Hogshead, "Asthma: Personal Stories: Nancy Hogshead, 1984 Olympic Gold Medalist," About.com, May 16, 2007. Reproduced by permission of A.D.A.M., Inc.

L ike many of you, I have asthma. Yes it is true: I, Nancy Hogshead, winner of three Olympic gold medals, have asthma—just like hundreds of others who have competed in the Olympics.

It was not easy preparing for the Olympics; I worked long and hard for more than ten years. My days would start with a swim at 5:30 A.M., and not end until I had worked out at least twice more. Good health was always in the forefront of my mind, since without my health I could not expect to win races. Athletes with asthma, who take care of their asthma as seriously as they attend to their training, have just as much of a chance of getting to the Olympics—not to mention winning the gold—as anyone else.

Olympic swimmer and asthma sufferer Nancy Hogshead won three gold medals in the 1984 Olympics. (Tony Duffy/Allsport/Getty Images)

Initial Disbelief

The first time a doctor asked me to get on a treadmill to test for asthma, I thought he was crazy. I thought people with asthma were sickly wheezers. I was a world champion swimmer, hardly a weakling. Sure, I was sick a lot and tended to cough during and after working out, but who doesn't breathe hard after an intense match against worthy opponents? But this doctor told me that people with asthma do not always wheeze (I did not), and that approximately ten percent of Olympic athletes from all over the world have asthma. He then gave me a list of the symptoms and I had almost all of them. I agreed to take the test, and was astonished to discover that when I really pushed it, I could be swimming with a 40% decrease in my lung capacity!

Being diagnosed with asthma was not the end of my asthma story; it was just the first step towards a healthier life. I was thrilled to learn that with a bronchodilator I could exercise without getting breathless (that is, no more breathless than I should get). But I still thought using my inhaler was something I could choose to do—or not do. I considered it a luxury, not a necessity. Do you know where that got me? Admitted to the hospital, unable to breathe and with pulled muscles in my back from coughing. I was even more frustrated because, for the first time, I knew that I did not have to be sick. If I had done what my doctor told me to do, I would never have been in that condition. It was a scary, miserable experience and one I promised myself I would never repeat.

The hospital experience taught me to make asthma management a part of my daily routine. But in order to truly control my asthma, I had to learn to monitor my condition and treat the smallest symptom quickly, even if I thought I felt fine. Slowly, I got better at associating small physical symptoms with asthma, and even learned

> **FAST FACT**
>
> Runner Jackie Joyner-Kersee and diver Greg Louganis are two other well-known Olympic champions with asthma.

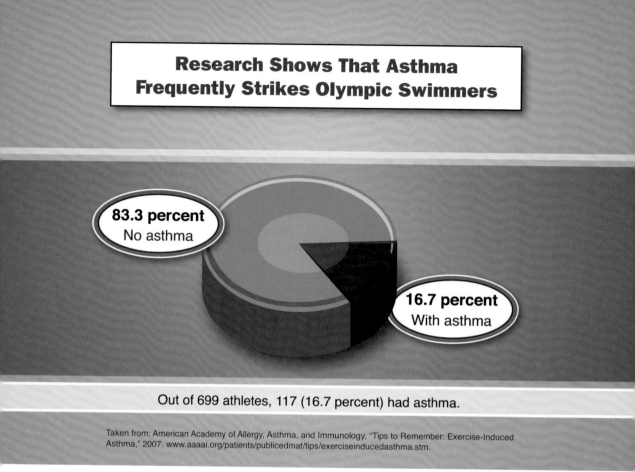

Research Shows That Asthma Frequently Strikes Olympic Swimmers

83.3 percent
No asthma

16.7 percent
With asthma

Out of 699 athletes, 117 (16.7 percent) had asthma.

Taken from: American Academy of Allergy, Asthma, and Immunology, "Tips to Remember: Exercise-Induced Asthma," 2007. www.aaaai.org/patients/publicedmat/tips/exerciseinducedasthma.stm.

how to predict when my peak flow reading was a little low. I learned that some medicines controlled my asthma better than others, and some made me sick. It was a year-long, trial-and-error process, but by sticking with it, I eventually found medicines that worked well for me, enabling me to go snow skiing even when the air was bitter cold. (Cold, dry air is one of my worst asthma triggers.) Having asthma is no reason to be sick. It may take a while, but if you work with your doctor, you'll find the best way to treat your asthma!

Getting Better All the Time

Most people are surprised to learn that I am healthier now than I was during the Olympics. That is because health does not just mean being in shape. I used to get what I thought were bronchitis and colds that kept me sick for more than a month each year. Before I knew about my asthma I was always struggling to catch my breath. I would frequently cough and sometimes pass out after a hard swim. Now that I know how to control my asthma, I don't have to miss out on even a single day. Working out became a more enjoyable experience for me because I no longer have to gasp for breath.

Your asthma should not bother you, and with proper diligent management, it won't. It may not be easy to achieve this, but it will put you—not your asthma, in control of your life. It doesn't mean just treating your symptoms when you have them, it means preventing the symptoms by doing something every day to maintain healthy lungs. Taking care of your asthma is like brushing your teeth: if you do it every day, you will rarely have problems.

I wish I had known about my asthma sooner, so I could have started feeling better sooner. Instead, I wasted a lot of time being frustrated when I got sick, instead of knowing how to prevent getting sick altogether.

A Parent's Tale of Coping with Her Children's Asthma

Denise Grady

All parents worry about their children's health. In the following selection Denise Grady tells of a concern that lasted throughout the childhood of her two sons. Born three years apart, Brian and Eric both developed asthma in their early years. They shared, as many asthmatics do, a number of allergic reactions that would trigger fits of coughing, wheezing, and difficulty in breathing. Moreover, colds and other nonallergic irritants could bring on an attack. Grady and her husband realized that they had a double duty as parents—to protect their children from asthma but also to protect them from feeling so fearful that they would not enjoy an ordinary childhood. With advice from their children's doctor and diligence in preventive care, they were able to succeed in walking that fine line. Grady is an award-winning science writer with *The New York Times.* She previously reported on science for *Time* and *Discover* magazines.

SOURCE: Denise Grady, "Learning to Live with Asthma: Two Young Brothers with the Same Chronic Illness," *Good Housekeeping,* vol. 245, August 2007, pp. 99–101. Copyright © 2007 Hearst Communications. Reproduced by permission.

When I first learned that my older son had asthma, I imagined that it would go away in a few weeks or months. I clung to that bit of denial, I guess, because it helped ease the fear and sadness as reality sank in. Brian was only 3, and deep down my husband and I knew we were facing a serious chronic disease that would probably hang on for years, maybe even for the rest of his life.

It did hang on, and three years later, our younger son, Eric, also started to wake up at night with fits of coughing, wheezing, and choking. Both boys had a cluster of problems—asthma, eczema, and allergies to nuts, pollens, dust mites, and animals—that often go together and seem to have become more common in the past 20 years or so.

A Killer of Children

People with asthma are often described as having "twitchy" lungs, hypersensitive to all kinds of irritants that don't bother others. The disease causes the airways to constrict temporarily and fill up with mucus, making it hard to breathe. Lots of things can trigger attacks: allergies, viruses, cigarette smoke, gas fumes, cold air, exercise, even laughing.

At least six million children in the United States have asthma. Worldwide, it affects about 300 million adults and children; 255,000 die from it each year, and deaths could increase by 20 percent over the next decade, reports the World Health Organization [WHO].

In this country, asthma rates in children climbed about 60 percent between 1980 and 2003, says the Centers for Disease Control and Prevention [CDC]. In kids under 5, the rates rose even more, jumping 160 percent from 1980 to 1994.

Our sons, born in 1984 and 1987, were part of this dismal trend; a surprising number of our friends and neighbors had children in the same boat. We didn't remember there being so many kids with asthma when we were young. Everything from air pollutants to obesity has been blamed for the surge, but researchers have yet to arrive at definitive explanations. My husband and I realized that we had two jobs: keeping our boys well and teaching them to take care of themselves when they were off with friends or at school and we weren't around to remind them to use their inhalers.

We also felt we had to walk a fine line. We wanted our sons to be cautious but not afraid, to take asthma seriously and yet not become obsessive or hypochondriacal. We didn't want them to be like the goofy neighbor kid who squirted his inhaler at classmates for laughs—or like the one whose parents kept him home at the first sign of a cough. We weren't really sure how to find a happy medium, except to be calm but insistent about doing what was needed to keep the disease under control.

We were fortunate to find our way to pediatricians who were good teachers, and we learned a number of things from them that turned out to be important for the long haul.

A Doctor's Stern Advice

My first lesson came when I mentioned that I knew parents who seemed to rush to the emergency room an awful lot because of their child's asthma attacks. Our normally mild-mannered pediatrician became irate and insisted there should be no need for emergency treatment—not if the asthma was being managed properly. His indignation made an impression on me. So did the idea that if we kept our wits about us, it might be possible to avoid trips to the emergency room.

I paid attention when he explained that even though our sons' asthma attacks occurred mainly at night, it would take several doses of medicine during the day, every day—even when they were feeling fine—to prevent the attacks. Initially, I found that hard to accept. Why couldn't they just take medicine at bedtime to get them

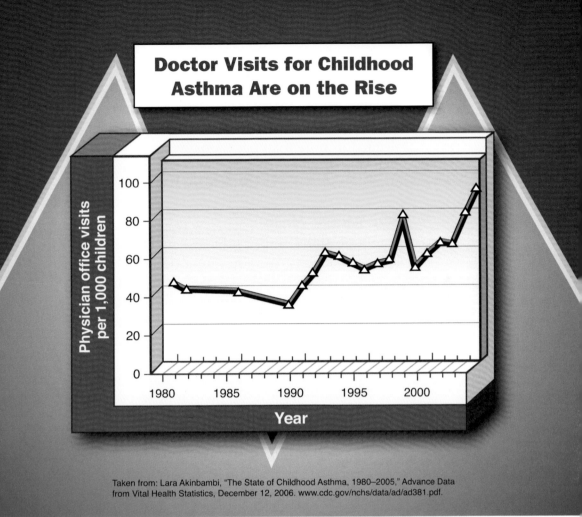

Doctor Visits for Childhood Asthma Are on the Rise

Physician office visits per 1,000 children

Year

Taken from: Lara Akinbambi, "The State of Childhood Asthma, 1980–2005," Advance Data from Vital Health Statistics, December 12, 2006. www.cdc.gov/nchs/data/ad/ad381.pdf.

through the night? I soon found out it wasn't enough. Like most parents, I hated the idea of giving my children drugs day after day, with no end in sight. Although there didn't seem to be immediate side effects, I wondered if problems might develop later, perhaps ones that hadn't even been discovered yet.

But we didn't really have a choice. Without the drugs, our sons had asthma attacks nearly every night. We followed all the crazy-making advice about buying special dust-mite-proof covers for mattresses and pillows, banishing pets, and getting rid of carpets and stuffed toys to keep dust away. But the only thing that clearly made a difference was asthma medicine. . . .

Guided by our doctors, we used various preventive drugs as the backbone of treatment. Most of the time, we used albuterol only to treat attacks. And if our sons needed it more than occasionally, we took that as a sign that they also needed more of the inflammation-fighting drugs.

Flu Shots Help

Viral infections, sinus problems, and allergies seemed to bring on attacks. We also found out, the hard way, that the flu can play havoc with asthma, and at a pediatrician's urging, we all started getting flu shots every year when the boys were in elementary school. It was one of the best decisions we ever made.

When the kids were young, we spent a lot of time showing them how to use inhalers and making sure they did it right. I don't have asthma, but I practiced with an inhaler anyway so that I could help them learn. It's amazingly easy to do it wrong and have the medicine land at the back of your throat or on the roof of your mouth instead of in your lungs. When the boys were younger, they used a device called a spacer, which attaches to the inhaler, captures the mist in a chamber, and makes the inhaler a bit easier to use.

All this practice turned out to be time well spent, because it helped make taking the medicine into a routine and a habit. The boys used inhalers at school or in public places if they needed to. We felt strongly that they had to carry their inhalers around, rather than stowing them in a teacher's desk or a nurse's office. Fortunately, the schools agreed.

Like most kids, our sons were always ready to argue, bargain, and negotiate over just about anything—bedtime, TV, sleepovers, computer games. But taking

> ## FAST FACT
>
> Some researchers believe that frequent exposure to chlorine in the air surrounding indoor pools can explain the rise of childhood asthma. They point to evidence from Europe, where asthma rates go up in step with the number of indoor pools.

the medicine wasn't an issue: It never even came up. I think it was clear that there was nothing to debate, and they were smart enough to know that the drugs were helping them.

Aiming for a Normal Childhood

They never missed school because of asthma, and we tried hard to keep the disease from interfering with their lives. When the boys wanted to play sports, we were delighted. They swam, played soccer and basketball, and in high school, both were track and cross-country runners. I can think of only one decision dictated by asthma: When Eric's elementary school was starting band classes, I asked the teacher not to assign him a wind instrument, because he'd been ill and I didn't think he had enough breath for a horn or a saxophone. We got lucky: Eric

Parents of asthmatic children must balance their children's asthma treatments with the need for the children to enjoy as ordinary a childhood as possible. (© **Aaron Flaum/Alamy**)

found out he loved percussion, and he still plays drums in a band in college.

Gradually, the asthma diminished for both of our sons, but Brian still has occasional attacks and can't afford to ignore respiratory infections, even ones that seem minor; he had a bout with pneumonia during his freshman year in college and needed an inhaler for the first time in years. That illness was a sobering reminder to all of us that although asthma loosened its grip over time, it never did let go entirely.

From Olympian to Congressman, with Asthma

Jim Ryun

If Jim Ryun was no good at sports as a kid, there may have been a reason. The young Ryun was asthmatic and did not know it, he explains in the following viewpoint. But despite his difficulties, he made the cross-country team in high school, and his coach recognized the root of his troubles. During a visit to the doctor, Ryun was made to realize that he suffered from allergies and asthma—the former contributing to the severity of the latter. He began to see a specialist, who administered allergy shots. Relieved of the triggers for his asthma, Ryun went on to set a new world record for the fastest mile when he was just twenty-one. During the 1968 Olympics, however, he had a setback. The games were held in Mexico City, a location that is known for its heavy air pollution. Ryun had an asthma attack so severe that he felt he might die. With treatment, he got over it, but in three Olympics he never won a gold medal. After his running career and a stint running sports camps, he was elected to Congress from a district in Kansas in 1996. He lost his seat in the 2006 election.

SOURCE: Jim Ryun, "Asthma: Personal Stories: Former U.S. Rep. Jim Ryun—'64, '68, '72 Olympics," University of Pennsylvania Health System, May 16, 2007. www.pennhealth.com. Copyright © 2007 A.D.A.M. Inc. Reproduced by permission.

I never dreamed when I was a young man that one day I would compete in the Olympics, break three world records, and be a life-long athlete. These are extraordinary accomplishments, even more so because I have exercise-induced asthma. Asthma has been part of my life for a long time, but I never let it stop me from doing the things I wanted to do.

As a child, I was never good at sports. I tried out for team after team, and as each one cut me, I grew increasingly frustrated with myself. Then I tried out for the cross-country team, and everything changed. Not only did I make the team, but I excelled at the sport. That spring I learned the incredible rush of winning a race. I also learned that I had asthma.

Despite having asthma, viewpoint author and track star Jim Ryun set world records for running the mile and completed in the 1964, 1968, and 1972 Olympic Games. (AP Images)

I had never heard of exercise-induced asthma before. I had assumed my breathlessness during and after exercise came from being out-of-shape. Fortunately for me, my coach knew enough to take me to an ear, nose, and throat doctor. He tested me for allergies, and it turned out I had lots of them. The doctor explained that allergies contribute to asthma, and he cautioned me to avoid allergens as much as possible. He also told me to "steam" my airways open at night, since at that time (early 1960s) there were not many asthma medications.

Asthma Cannot Stop a Runner Forever

Within 3 months of cross-country training, it was clear that the Lord had given me a talent to run and to run fast. By my senior year, I was one of the top high school runners in the U.S. and a member of the U.S. Olympic team. In just two years, I went from being an average high school student to a national sports star. The pressure (and I don't mean sinus pressure) was enormous. Suddenly I had to worry about pleasing not only myself and my parents, but my coach, my teammates, the press, and my country.

In 1967, I started taking allergy shots. I was 21 years old and training for the 1968 Olympics. I was seeing an allergist who worked with athletes, and he suggested I try the shots. That same year, I became the fastest person to ever run one mile, with a time of 3 minutes, 51.1 seconds. That record held for 8 years. I don't know for certain if the allergy shots helped me break the world record, but I know they certainly helped me breathe better. I have felt much better since I started taking allergy shots.

Things seemed to be going well. My asthma did not make me different from any other member of the team, except that I had to bring my own pillows on trips and arrange to get my allergy shots in other cities. Then, during

> ## FAST FACT
>
> Asthma seems to be especially common among runners. One study found that 56 percent of recreational road runners showed allergy and asthma symptoms.

Runners with Allergies Tend to Have Asthma

In a study of elite runners, asthma-like symptoms were strongly associated with allergies. Of the runners with allergies, 75 percent (30 of 40) had symptoms, compared with 37 percent (23 of 60) of the runners without allergies.

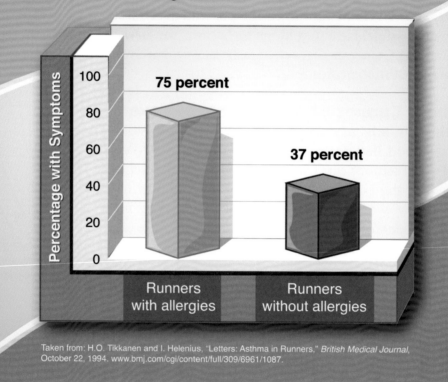

Taken from: H.O. Tikkanen and I. Helenius, "Letters: Asthma in Runners," *British Medical Journal*, October 22, 1994. www.bmj.com/cgi/content/full/309/6961/1087.

the 1968 Olympics in Mexico City, I had a big scare. I had just finished running in my final race and was walking back to the finish line. I don't remember exactly what happened in the next few minutes, but I was suddenly aware that I couldn't breathe. I couldn't breathe at all. To make matters worse, I couldn't find anyone who spoke English. Somehow I got medical help and everything was okay. Looking back on it, I should have realized that I was in a city known for its high levels of air pollution and high elevation (7,400 feet above sea level). Add the intense race I had just run, and you have the makings of an asthma attack. That experience really shook me up.

I no longer run competitively, but I still enjoy running, and I still have to take care of my asthma. My wife, Anne, and I keep a dust-free home. I continue to take allergy shots and use an air filter. I'm fortunate that I can keep my asthma under control by keeping my allergies under control. After years of representing the U.S. in international events, I had the honor of representing my home state, Kansas, in the U.S. Congress. I am extremely proud of my accomplishments as a sportsman and as a statesman, and grateful to the Lord for enabling me to serve our nation. Everyone faces obstacles in life, and asthma is one that can be overcome by paying attention to your body and taking your symptoms seriously.

Learning What It Is Like to Be Asthmatic

Vincent McGovern

In the following selection Vincent McGovern describes his memories of poorly controlled asthma. As a child, McGovern suffered from many attacks and had limited treatment options. But, as he has found through the years, asthma is controllable and manageable. He also relates that he believes doctors and general practitioners who have suffered or known someone who has suffered from asthma are more sympathetic to asthmatic patients. McGovern is a clinical assistant in adult chest medicine at Belfast City Hospital and in pediatric asthma at Royal Belfast Hospital for Sick Children in Northern Ireland.

I developed asthma around the age of two. It wasn't a difficult diagnosis: recurrent cough and wheeze in a child covered in atopic eczema with a family history of asthma. In any case I never grew out of it, so it couldn't have been wheezy bronchitis!

That was the early 1960s. Treatment options were very limited and I was prescribed Tedral syrup. Now we know

SOURCE: Vincent McGovern, "Learning from Illness: I Know How Frightening Asthma Can Be," *Pulse,* August 2, 2004. Copyright © 2004 CPM Information Ltd. Reproduced by permission.

that such theophylline preparations can cause nausea— I suffered nausea and retching just trying to swallow the syrup. Still that's all there was in those days and drastic times called for drastic measures.

I experienced intermittent, but significant, flare-ups of asthma throughout my childhood, and these had a significant impact on my life.

As a boy I was out on the street playing football from the minute I arrived home from school. There were no computer games in those days and we played on until way after dark. I usually started playing with no symptoms, but always ended up wheezing in goal. There is a myth about asthmatics wanting to be goalkeepers—we usually start playing outfield and only end up in goal when we can't breathe.

In those days my asthma attacks were very frequent. I can remember them happening late at night, visits from the GP [general practitioner physician] by the light of the bedside table, and injections into my arm which could only have been aminophylline. I remember when the GP was called out after dark, there was always a new bar of soap and clean towel left out for him. There seemed to be more fuss being made about the doctor having to come out than there was about my asthma attack. How times have changed!

The Burden of Asthma Attacks

As a child asthma attacks were very emotional for me. I can remember one particularly bad attack that left me sitting hunched forward in the middle of the living room with my distressed family surrounding me. I was sobbing uncontrollably and bidding my parents farewell, thanking them for everything they had done for me and convinced that my next breath was going to be my last. At the age of 11 my GP prescribed an Intal Spinhaler, an early dry powder device. Looking back now I realise how clued in my GP was—such treatment was a real innovation back

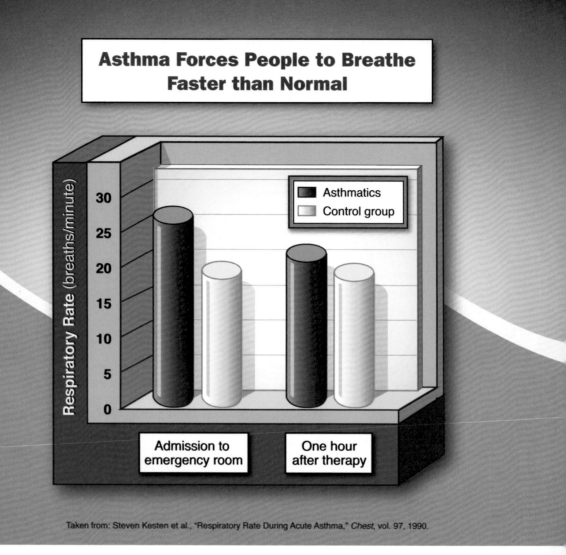

Asthma Forces People to Breathe Faster than Normal

Respiratory Rate (breaths/minute)

30
25
20
15
10
5
0

Asthmatics
Control group

Admission to emergency room

One hour after therapy

Taken from: Steven Kesten et al., "Respiratory Rate During Acute Asthma," *Chest*, vol. 97, 1990.

then. Intal Spincaps were supposed to be a preventive, but I soon worked out that the isoprenaline of the Intal Compound Spincaps provided great relief!

My teens were punctuated by repeated flare-ups, with resulting rounded shoulders. Image is everything as a teenager but the figure-of-eight support [back brace] I bought from a Sunday newspaper to improve my posture stood no chance against my poorly controlled asthma.

During my A-levels [advanced studies] nocturnal waking became a regular occurrence. My doctor told me it was a stress-related exacerbation and prescribed diazepam, which stopped the wakenings—at least I think it did but maybe I just slept through them.

As a newly-qualified doctor in my 20s, I became the 'Ventolin inhaler in every pocket, coat and orifice' kind of asthmatic. I checked my peakflows diligently; they were 400L/min, dipping most nights to 250L/min with Ventolin needed from the bedside table. If ever I discovered I had left home without my inhaler I would always have to go back for it, no matter how far I had travelled.

Improvements

It wasn't until 1989 that a pharmaceutical company rep persuaded me that inhaled steroids would make a difference. Within weeks the night-time wakings had gone

"The Air Experience" simulator, manufactured by the biomedicine company Genentech, gives the participant the feeling of breathlessness and the ensuing panic that asthmatics experience every day. (© Alexandra Buhl/Alamy)

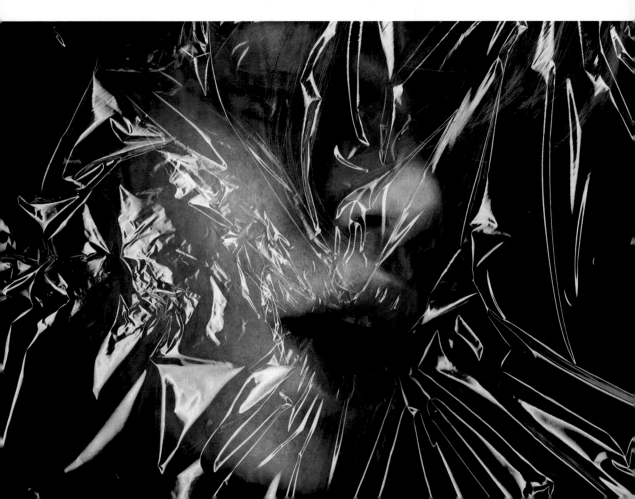

and my need for Ventolin was dramatically reduced. My peakflow stabilised between 400–440 L/min [liters per minute]—still not great but I was very grateful for the dramatic improvement in my quality of life.

A few years later I added in a long-acting bronchodilator and my peak flows rose to 520. My need for Ventolin disappeared almost overnight and my asthma was no longer exacerbated by exercise.

We now know that low-dose inhaled steroids and long-acting bronchodilators work very well together. I have been on a combination inhaler for a while now. I rarely get symptoms, do not have exercise intolerance and hardly ever need my blue inhaler. My compliance is good; I take my inhaler every morning without fail and I have learnt over the years that it keeps me well.

But, it's clear to me that 30 years of unopposed asthma inflammation have taken their toll on my lungs. Re-modelling does occur and I think I now have some degree of chronic irreversible airflow obstruction. I just hope the ongoing treatment will prevent the damage from worsening now my symptoms are well controlled.

Asthma Can Be Managed

So do asthmatic doctors or doctors with asthmatic children tend to treat the condition more sympathetically? You bet they do! Only someone who suffers from asthma can understand the impact the symptoms have on daily life—and what the fear of having an asthma attack really feels like.

The majority of asthmatics have mild to moderate disease, which can be controlled by appropriate, enthusiastic, individually tailored treatment. Low-dose inhaled

> **FAST FACT**
>
> Many therapists believe that asthma patients can experience some relief of symptoms by undergoing training to alter their breathing patterns. However, a scientific review of studies finds no clear evidence that this helps, leaving the question open to further research.

steroids taken on a regular basis remain the cornerstone of management and where residual symptoms persist, additional therapy such as long-acting Beta$_2$-agonists can be added in to provide better control. Compliance with regular treatment remains a problem; patients have to be educated and persuaded to take regular treatment. The aims and benefits of doing so must be carefully explained.

I always ask patients the same series of questions to assess their disease control.

Too many patients and health care professionals have low expectations of what can realistically be achieved for the majority and treatment standards often fall far below what should be expected.

GLOSSARY

allergen   A normally harmless substance (such as a food or pollen) that causes an allergic reaction.

allergy   A faulty immune response to a normally harmless substance; a condition frequently associated with asthma.

alveoli   Tiny pouches at the ends of airways in the lungs where the exchange of oxygen and carbon dioxide takes place.

anti-inflammatory   Inflammation-reducing medication that helps reverse mucus production and swelling in the airways.

asthma   A chronic lung disease, characterized by inflammation and swelling of the airways (bronchial tubes).

beta-agonist   A medication that opens the airways of the lung by relaxing the muscles around the airways.

breathing rate   The number of breaths per minute.

bronchial tubes   The large airways that branch away from the end of the windpipe.

bronchioles   The small branches of the airways that connect bronchial tubes and alveoli (air sacs).

bronchodilator   Medication that relaxes the muscle bands around the airways (*see* beta agonist).

carbon dioxide   A colorless, odorless gas that is carried by the blood to the lungs to be exhaled.

chronic disease   A persistent disease that can be managed but not cured.

exhalation   The breathing of air out of the lungs.

inflammation	A bodily reaction to trauma, allergy, or other events that includes redness, swelling, and pain in a tissue.
inhalation	The breathing of air into the lungs.
inhaler	A handheld device that delivers a dose of bronchodilator into the lungs of an asthma patient.
lung function tests	Procedures that examine the performance and capacity of a patient's lungs.
nebulizer	A device that changes liquid medicine into an aerosol or mist for inhalation.
peak flow meter	A small handheld device that measures how fast air comes out of the lungs when a person exhales forcefully.
peak flow rate	A test used to measure how fast air can be exhaled from the lungs.
respiration	The exchange of oxygen and carbon dioxide by the movement of air in and out of the lungs.
spirometry	A breathing test that measures the rate and volume of air moving through the lungs.
steroid	A type of medication used to reduce swelling and inflammation in the lungs. Also called corticosteroid.
trachea	The main airway, also known as the windpipe.
triggers	Substances or events that initiate an asthma attack.
wheezing	A whistling sound produced by air moving through narrowed airways.

CHRONOLOGY

ca. 100   Greek physician Aretaeus of Cappadocia writes of maintaining health through *pneuma*, or "vital air," which some have interpreted as a reference to battling asthma.

ca. 1150   Rabbi Moses Maimonides, a celebrated physician of the time, writes a treatise on the management of asthma for Prince al-Afdal.

1698   English physician John Floyer publishes the first book in English on the symptoms, causes, and treatment of asthma.

1903   Adrenaline, a form of epinephrine, becomes the first synthetic drug used to ease the symptoms of asthma.

1942   The American Academy of Allergy, Asthma & Immunology is founded.

1951   Isoetharine, a type of muscle relaxing drug known as a beta-agonist, is approved for treatment of asthma; however, it proves to have adverse effects on the heart.

1970   Congress adopts and President Nixon signs the Clean Air Act in response to the growing recognition that air pollution can harm respiratory health.

1980   A steep rise in childhood asthma begins, although it will be some years before the trend is recognized.

1995   After rising annually for fifteen years, the U.S. asthma prevalence rate among children appears to level off at 7.5 percent.

1997   The "hygiene hypothesis," which posits that excessive cleanliness causes asthma, is published in peer-reviewed journals.

1999   A new class of asthma drug treatments known as long-acting beta-agonists (LABAs) is introduced. Instead of reacting to the onset of symptoms, patients using a LABA inhale it daily to prevent attacks.

2007   A Food and Drug Administration Pediatric Advisory Committee calls into question the safety of LABAs for children.

2008   University of Wisconsin researchers discover that infants who develop severe colds caused by the rhinovirus have a greatly increased chance of developing asthma later in childhood.

ORGANIZATIONS TO CONTACT

The editors have compiled the following list of organizations concerned with the issues debated in this book. The descriptions are derived from materials provided by the organizations. All have publications or information available for interested readers. The list was compiled on the date of publication of the present volume; the information provided here may change. Be aware that many organizations take several weeks or longer to respond to inquiries, so allow as much time as possible.

American Academy of Allergy, Asthma & Immunology (AAAAI)
555 E. Wells St.
Ste. 1100
Milwaukee, WI
53202-3823
(414) 272-6071
www.aaaai.org

The AAAAI is the largest professional medical specialty organization in the United States, representing allergists, asthma specialists, clinical immunologists, allied health professionals, and others with a special interest in the research and treatment of allergic disease. Established in 1943, the AAAAI has more than six thousand members in the United States, Canada, and sixty other countries. The mission of the AAAAI is the advancement of the knowledge and practice of allergy, asthma, and immunology for optimal patient care.

American Academy of Nurse Practitioners (AANP)
PO Box 12846
Austin, TX 78711
(512) 442-4262
fax: (512) 442-6469
www.aanp.org

The AANP is the largest professional membership organization in the United States for nurse practitioners of all specialties, including asthma. The AANP strives to promote excellence in nurse practitioner practice, education, and research and to advance health policy that promotes access to high quality, cost effective health care for all.

American Association for Respiratory Care (AARC)
9425 N. MacArthur Blvd., Ste. 100
Irving, TX 75063-4706
(972) 243-2272
fax: (972) 484-2720
www.aarc.org

The AARC, a professional membership association of respiratory therapists, focuses primarily on respiratory therapy education and research. Its goals are to ensure that respiratory patients receive safe and effective care from qualified professionals and to benefit respiratory health-care providers. The association also advocates on behalf of pulmonary patients for appropriate access to respiratory services provided by qualified professionals.

American College of Allergy, Asthma & Immunology (ACAAI)
85 W. Algonquin Rd.
Ste. 550
Arlington Heights, IL 60005
(847) 427-1200
fax: (847) 427-1294
www.acaai.org

The ACAAI is a professional association of four thousand allergists and immunologists. Established in 1942, the association is dedicated to improving the quality of patient care in allergy and immunology through research, advocacy, and professional and public education. Among other goals, the ACAAI seeks to improve the quality of patient care in allergy, asthma, and immunology.

American College of Chest Physicians (ACCP)
3300 Dundee Rd.
Northbrook, Illinois 60062-2348
(847) 498-1400
www.chestnet.org

The ACCP is a leading resource for improvement in cardiopulmonary health. The ACCP seeks to promote the prevention and treatment of diseases of the chest through leadership, education, research, and communication. It publishes the journal *CHEST* among other publications, which frequently includes research articles on asthma.

American Lung Association
61 Broadway, 6th Fl.
New York, NY 10006
(212) 315-8700
www.lungusa.org

The American Lung Association is the leading organization working to prevent lung disease and promote lung health. The American Lung Association funds vital research on the causes of and treatments for lung disease, including asthma; advocates for clean air; and educates patients living with lung disease.

American Thoracic Society (ATS)
61 Broadway
New York, NY 10006-2755
(212) 315-8600
fax: (212) 315-6498
vvww.thoracic.org

The ATS, founded in 1905, is an independently incorporated international educational and scientific society that focuses on respiratory and critical care medicine. The society's approximately 13,500 members help prevent and fight respiratory disease around the globe through research, education, patient care, and advocacy.

Association of Asthma Educators (AAE)
1215 Anthony Ave.
Columbia, SC 29201-1701
(888) 988-7747
fax: (803) 254-3773
www.asthma
educators.org

The AAE aims to promote education as an integral component of a comprehensive asthma program, to raise the competence of the health-care professional who educates individuals and families affected by asthma, and to raise the standard of care and quality of asthma education delivered to those with asthma.

FOR FURTHER READING

Books

Francis V. Adams, *The Asthma Sourcebook.* New York: Mc-Graw-Hill, 2007.

Sayed Hasan Arshad, *Asthma.* New York: Oxford University Press, 2009.

Peter J. Barnes et al., *Asthma and COPD: Basic Mechanisms and Clinical Management.* Boston: Elsevier/Academic Press, 2009.

William E. Berger and Jackie Joyner-Kersee, *Asthma for Dummies.* Hoboken: John Wiley & Sons, 2004.

Christopher H. Fanta, Lynda M. Cristiano, and Kenan Hayer, *The Harvard Medical School Guide to Taking Control of Asthma.* New York: Simon & Schuster, 2003.

Jean Ford, *Breathe Easy! A Teen's Guide to Allergies and Asthma.* Broomall, PA: Mason Crest, 2005.

Stephen T. Holgate and Jo Douglas, *Fast Facts: Asthma.* Abingdon, NJ: Health Press, 2006.

Massoud Mahmoudi, *Allergy and Asthma: Practical Diagnosis and Management.* New York: McGraw-Hill Medical, 2008.

Claudia S. Plottel, *100 Questions About Your Child's Asthma.* Sudbury, MA: Jones & Bartlett, 2008.

John Rees and Dipak Kanabar, *ABCs of Asthma.* Malden, MA: Blackwell, 2006.

Rae Simons, *Why Can't I Breathe: Kids and Asthma.* Vestal, New York: AlphaHouse, 2009.

Peter Paul Van Asperen, *When Your Child Has Asthma.* New York: Simon and Schuster, 2007.

Periodicals

American Thoracic Society, "Asthma Risk Higher in Babies Born During Fall," *EmaxHealth*, November 21, 2009. www.emaxhealth.com.

American Thoracic Society, "More Pounds Equals Worse Asthma?" *ScienceDaily*, May 23, 2007. www.sciencedaily.com.

Allan B. Becker, "Asthma in the Preschool Child: Still a Rose by Any Other Name?" *Journal of Allergy and Clinical Immunology*, December 2008.

Jack Michael Becker, James Rogers, Gregory Rossini, Haresh Mirchandani, and Gilbert E. D'alonzo, "Asthma Deaths During Sports: Report of a Seven-Year Experience," *Journal of Allergy and Clinical Immunology*, January 2002.

Blythe Bernard, "St. Louis Is Worst Place to Live for People with Asthma," *St. Louis Post Dispatch*, January 28, 2009. www.stltoday.com.

Peyton A. Eggleston, "The Environment and Asthma in US Inner Cities," *Chest*, November 2007.

Amanda Gardner, "FDA Finds No Link So Far Between Asthma Drugs and Suicide Risk," *HealthDayNews*, January 14, 2009. www.hon.ch/News/HSN/623089.html.

Serena Gordon, "Common Asthma Treatments Don't Work for Virus-Induced Wheeze," *HealthDay*, January 21, 2009. www.healthday.com/Article.asp?AID=623315.

Moira Inkelas et al., "Race/Ethnicity, Language, and Asthma Care: Findings from a 4-State Survey," *Annals of Allergy, Asthma & Immunology*, January 2008.

Greg Lavine, "FDA Still Examining Potential Link Between Certain Asthma Drugs, Suicidality," American Society of Health-System Pharmacists, January 16, 2009. www.ashp.org.

Mayo Clinic, "Increased Risk of Pneumococcal Disease Found in Asthma Patients," *EmaxHealth*, December 20, 2008. www.emaxhealth.com.

Kathi McNaughton, "Understanding Cough Variant Asthma," *HealthCentral.com*, February 1, 2009.

Jennifer Newbould et al., "'I'm Fine Doing It on My Own': Partnerships Between Young People and Their Parents in the Management of Medication for Asthma and Diabetes," *Journal of Child Health Care*, June 2008.

Claire O'Boyle, "Agony over Birthday Asthma Attack Boy Killed by Excitement," *Daily Mirror*, February 7, 2009. www.mirror .co.uk.

January W. Payne, "So Long, 2008, and Farewell, Cheap Asthma Inhalers," *U.S. News & World Report*, December 31, 2008. www .usnews.com.

Ginger Rough, "Researchers Find Way to Cut Ozone's Effects on Asthma," *Arizona Republic*, February 4, 2009. www.azcentral .com.

Rachel Stults, "Vanderbilt Researchers Link Cold Virus to Asthma," *Tennessean*, February 9, 2009. www.tennessean.com.

University of Virginia Health System, "Chronic Asthma: Study Reveals Long-Lasting Airway Blockages, Even in Medicated Asthma Patients," *ScienceDaily*, February 6, 2009.

Carly Weeks, "One-Third of Asthma Cases May Be Misdiagnosed, Study Says," *Globe and Mail* (Toronto), November 17, 2009. www.theglobeandmail.com.

Todd Zwillich, "FDA Panel Urges Restrictions on 2 Asthma Drugs," *MedicineNet.com*, December 11, 2009. www.medicine net.com.

INDEX